W9-DHJ-880

A PICTORIAL HISTORY
OF THE WESTERN FILM

A PICTORIAL

HISTORY OF THE WESTERN FILM

By WILLIAM K. EVERSON

THE CITADEL PRESS — NEW YORK

ACKNOWLEDGMENTS

For their unstinting cooperation in many ways, but especially for supplying many of the rarest stills in this volume, I wish to thank James Card, motion picture curator of the George Eastman House in Rochester, N.Y., and producer Alex Gordon

Grateful thanks are also extended to George Pratt of the George Eastman House; Jacques Ledoux of the Royal Film Archive, Belgium; Janus Barfoed of the Danish Film Archive; and William Kenly of Paramount Pictures.

First paperbound edition, 1971
Copyright © 1969 by William K. Everson
All rights reserved
Published by Citadel Press, Inc., a subsidiary of Lyle Stuart, Inc.
222 Park Avenue South, New York, N.Y. 10003
In Canada: George J. McLeod Limited
73 Bathurst Street, Toronto 2B, Ontario
Manufactured in the United States of America
Designed by A. Christopher Simon
ISBN 0-8065-0257-6

Dedicated to my children, Bambi and Griffith,
who, born and raised in an era of super-spies and rocketships,
still appreciate and prefer William S. Hart and Gene Autry

CONTENTS

AN INTRODUCTION TO SEVENTY YEARS OF WESTERNS   1

1

THE BEGINNINGS — AND BRONCHO BILLY   14

2

PIONEERS OF AN ART: D. W. GRIFFITH AND THOMAS H. INCE   23

3

WILLIAM S. HART   37

4

JOHN FORD: A HALF-CENTURY OF HORSE OPERAS 46

5

THE PRE–1920's — AND TOM MIX 57

6

THE FIRST EPICS 70

7

STARS OF THE TWENTIES 80

8

THE COMING OF SOUND 108

9

THE "B" BOOM 124

10

THE THIRTIES 154

11

THE FORTIES — A PEAK OF POPULARITY 172

12

THE FIFTIES — AND RADICAL CHANGES 201

13

THE SIXTIES: WESTERNS, WESTERNS EVERYWHERE, BUT... 225

INDEX 242

A PICTORIAL HISTORY
OF THE WESTERN FILM

AN INTRODUCTION TO
SEVENTY YEARS OF WESTERNS

As these introductory notes are written, the Western film is well over seventy years old. During that considerable span it has undergone continual changes of emphasis to appeal to a juvenile audience in one era, an adult one in another. It has had to adjust to technological changes within the film and reshape itself to fight off the inflation of rising production costs. It has seen itself apparently bite the dust on the theatre screen only to be reincarnated on television. It has even seen itself produced en masse in Germany, Yugoslavia, and Spain. The Europeans have seen the Western as a major contribution to American art and culture, as integral a part of American folklore as the Odyssey is of the Greeks'. And to American audiences, the Western, whatever its

form—humble "B" feature, grand-scale epic in color and widescreen, or thirty-minute television potboiler—has always remained one of the most reliable staples of movie entertainment. Regardless of super-heroes and spacemen, there is a period in every child's life when a cowboy on a galloping horse is the most exciting vision imaginable; and as long as the John Fords and the Henry Kings (and, of course, the John Waynes) are there to wrest poetry, beauty, and drama from a fairly restricted genre, the Western will work its magic on the adult too. Perhaps the most surprising thing is not that Hollywood has been able to draw such variety and inspiration from one geographic location and a set of rigid clichés, but that it has been able to do so, to the tune of thousands of films, for so long. Germany, after all, has made but intermittent use of its Wagnerian legends as film material; Britain's parallel to the Jesse James era, its Robin Hood period, has admittedly been well-exploited cinematically, but nowhere to the same extent as American western history, while its colorful Civil War (King Charles I versus Cromwell) has been almost totally ignored, even though it contains the same potential for drama, action and sentiment as America's Civil War. Yet for seventy years now, the American movie has made box-office hay out of the "Wild West"—a period surrounding and containing the rise of the great cattle empires, and in terms of duration, less than half the time-span already devoted to it by the movies.

Despite this long and honorable history, however, the Western as a genre has never been accorded the respect it really deserves. The critics will rightly praise the beauty of a major John Ford production, and then dismiss the great mass of remaining films with an "if you've seen one, you've seen them all" sneer and a snide summing-up of alleged clichés. But when one tries to pin down these clichés, it is amazing how elusive they can be. A major TV network, doing a documentary on the Western a few years back, thought it might be fun to edit together a number of scenes of a character pointing off-screen and telling the sheriff, "They went thattaway!" as being the epitome of clichéd Western story-telling. But while it's a useful line by which the uninformed can "prove" their point, it isn't a line that has really been used that much, and the television documentary, after much fruitless screening, had to get along without it. If there *is* one key line that the "B" Westerns have used incessantly, it is that classic last-reel resolution by the defeated villains, "Let's get outta here!" But it doesn't

THE GUN: George Barnes in
The Great Train Robbery
(Edison, 1903)

2

have the same easy Western ring to it as "They went thattaway!" and its omnipresence in so many Westerns would in any case not be apparent to critics, who rarely see the "B" products.

As recently as April, 1969, a New York *Sunday News* article on the changing styles in the Western commented that contemporary movie cowboys are ". . . non-heroes and obsessed by sex . . . ," a statement that ignores the fact that with the possible exception of John Wayne, there are no more movie cowboys as such, merely actors (Brando, Fonda, Holden) who occasionally appear in individual Westerns. The same article, summing up the old-time cowboy hero in one convenient if inaccurate phrase, added that in earlier days "the hero would kiss his faithful horse and ride off alone into the sunset." This again is a fallacy that has been repeated so many times that it has been accepted as part of the unwritten law ruling the making of Westerns, but it just isn't supported by the facts. William S. Hart, it is true, had a deep affection for his horses, partly because it came naturally to him, and partly because he recognized the very real comradeship between a man and his horse in the early days of the West, and tried to show it in his movies. But he rarely kissed his horse in a movie, and then only in moments of such dramatic stress (when he had been rejected by humans, leaving his horse as his only true friend, or when, as in *Pinto Ben,* the horse was dying) that such an emotional gesture would be acceptable. But Hart certainly never once kissed his horse before riding off alone into the sunset, or as a substitute for feminine caresses. Hart's leading ladies were always well and truly kissed, usually well before the fadeout. Furthermore, he was such a romanticist that the number of films in which he died, or rode off alone for the fade-

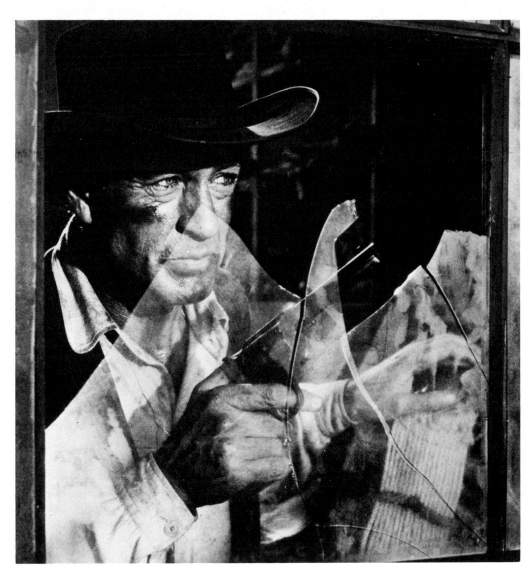

THE GUN: Gary Cooper in *High Noon* (United Artists, 1952)

3

THE CRIME: George Barnes in *The Great Train Robbery* (Edison, 1903)

out, were very much in the minority, and he usually wound up with the heroine as his bride. This, in fact, applies to almost all of the cowboy heroes, since the heroine's love was the only concrete reward they could hope to gain for all of their Herculean labors and courage.

Romance, certainly, was seldom stressed in Westerns, any more than it was in the equally innocent comedies of Harold Lloyd, Harry Langdon and Buster Keaton. But it was present, often a definite plot motivation, and most of the cowboy heroes kissed their heroines if not regularly, then at least frequently. Stars like Buck Jones who made fairly realistic Westerns and had an adult as well as juvenile following never had any qualms about a climactic kiss. The other stars, whose appeal was more to juveniles and who followed a very rigid code of conduct, tended to apologize for their lack of romantic ardor by making a joke of it. While Gene Autry did kiss Irene Manning in one of his earlier Westerns, thereafter

he saw to it that any such activity took place off-screen or quite inadvertently, as when he and his leading lady would be pushed into an embrace by the nudgings of an obliging and match-making horse.

Another cliché that has been much misunderstood (and its application exaggerated) is that of the white-Stetsoned hero and the black-hatted villain. Admittedly, such distinctions are an easy way of symbolizing good and evil, but this line of reasoning doesn't hold much water when one realizes just how many *heroes* have used black as their basic costume color too. (At one time a moustache was equally a dead giveaway as to its wearer's villainous and probably also lecherous make-up.) There were subtler differences than just the contrast between black and white. The villain's clothes, for example, were usually well-tailored, often ostentatious, implying an affluence which (since it was not shared by other townspeople, who were compelled to dress in standard Western garb) could only be supported by

4

THE CRIME: Walter Miller in *Fugitive Sheriff* (Columbia, 1936)

illicit activity. Distinctive costuming made it easier to keep tabs on who was who in the long shots and fast-action scenes, it made it simpler to use doubles without the deception becoming obvious (a wide-brimmed hat can hide an awful lot of face!), and too, it made it possible to re-use footage in later films, if the new actors wore matching clothes.

Considering the fairly standardized action content of the Western—the chase, the fist-fight, the gun duel, the stampede—it is surprising how so few basic ingredients have been pressed into service to flesh out a dozen or more other basics in actual plot-lines. Far from being all the same, the Western has in fact managed to offer far more story variation than its Japanese parallel, the Samurai film. The pioneering themes—the wagon train or cattle herd trek or the building of a railroad—have of course occupied a large percentage of the plots. But most of the story-lines have depended on villainy for their precise motivation, since the hero's activities have

remained quite constant. And when the villain's perfidy included a lecherous yen for the heroine (oddly enough, he was usually sufficiently conventional to want to marry her, despite her obvious distaste for him) then a little more variety was added.

Discounting the pioneering and epic themes, most Western plots fall into one of twelve groups. First, of course, there is the Sin Town masterminded by the villain from his gambling casino. Despite the enormous profits from his always crooked games, he can't resist such extra-curricular activities as stage-robbing, cattle-rustling and claim-jumping. This kind of catch-all plot allowed for both a straightforward action approach, or a semi-historical foray which tried to parallel the activities of Wyatt Earp or Bat Masterson. Dodge City, Deadwood, Nevada City, Wichita, Tombstone, Brimstone, Waco and a dozen other frontier helltowns were cleaned up a score of times by Hollywood heroes ranging from Richard Dix to Roy Rogers.

5

More often than not, however, the villain was more of a specialist, with a specific aim in view. Establishing a vast cattle empire (and in so doing, terrorizing all the other ranchers so that they'd move out or sell out) was an idea that was more a specialty of the villains of bigger Westerns (Joseph Calleia in *Wyoming*) although by no means beyond the range of lesser names. However, carving an empire required a certain dignity and polish; among the "B" Western heavies, Walter Miller could get away with it—but Fred Kohler couldn't.

Sometimes an element of mystery might creep in, with even the hero baffled by the meaningless killings and reigns of terror designed to force ranchers off their apparently worthless land. Audiences however, knew that the solution would have to be one of three possibilities: one section of land controlled the water for the valley, and the heavy was after total acquisition of all the water rights; gold or other mineral deposits had been discovered by the villain on land other than his own; or, and this was the most likely, the railroad was about to come through and it was imperative that the heavy own the entire district, so that the railroad would be forced to pay his price.

The deliberate sabotaging of progress made the villain

THE COSTUME: William S. Hart and Louise Glaum (Triangle, 1916)

THE SATIRE:
Ben Turpin and Phyllis Haver
in *Small Town Idol*
(First National, 1921)

6

THE COSTUME: Roy Rogers and Jane Frazee (Republic, 1950)

doubly despicable: unpatriotic as well as greedy. He might be wrecking the telegraph lines to protect his own stagecoach (and news-carrying) business, or he might be out to prevent the honest citizens from voting their territory into the Union, knowing that such a move would bring law and order, and an end to his profitable regime.

The simplest plot device of all of course was for the Texas Ranger or U.S. marshal hero to pose as a badman, join the outlaw gang, and work from the inside to bring about their downfall—a gimmick that added suspense to the normal action values and was valid enough to work in big city crime thrillers too.

Republic Pictures in particular was especially fond of what one might term the "Reconstruction" Western—stories set in the immediate post-Civil War period, with corrupt politicians and guerillas legally taking over defeated territories, and plundering them via excessive taxes. Republic used this one basic plot scores of times for all of its Western heroes.

Stirring up the Indians was another old reliable. Since the basic villainy was centered in the white trader or crooked Indian agent who plied the redmen with liquor and guns and assured them that the Great White Father

THE SATIRE:
Abbott & Costello, Douglas Dumbrille, and Iron Eyes Cody in *Ride 'Em Cowboy* (Universal, 1942)

in Washington spoke with a forked tongue, it was easy to use the Indians (and inexpensive stock shots) for all sorts of mayhem, and then send them on their way, somewhat decimated, at the end of the film with an understanding pat on the head, the white heavy having by then received his just deserts.

Having the hero returning (or escaping) from jail to prove his innocence and trap the real culprits was a ploy used mainly by the more serious Western stars, such as Buck Jones and George O'Brien. Others, like William Boyd and Gene Autry, with a more predominantly juvenile audience, were anxious to avoid having their heroes burdened, even if innocently, with a jailbird stigma. And in any case, such plots usually required a

the Army, invariably led to a race between the equipment and horses of the good guys and those of the villains (who of course, had an ample supply of henchmen like Edmund Cobb and Tom London to sabotage their opponents). Such themes were especially popular at Republic, since their climactic excitement provided a field day for Yakima Canutt and his unique organization of stuntmen.

And last but far from least, there was another old faithful—the hero's determined search for the murderer of his father. This theme became almost a fetish with Bob Steele, who in picture after picture grew to manhood relentlessly seeking revenge. In *The Man From Hell's Edges* it seemed that he had struck a distinctly

THE OFT-FILMED TALE: Chester Morris, Lewis Stone, and Walter Brennan in *Three Godfathers* (MGM, 1936)

little more serious acting as the hero faced local ostracism, which in turn reduced the action potential too.

There was a lot of mileage to be gained from family feuds and range wars between sheepmen and cattlemen. Few Westerns had the sheer guts of *To the Last Man* (a Zane Grey adaptation), which made no bones about two clans hating each other and ultimately wiping each other out. Usually the ploy was to have an unknown villain prodding the feud along for his own selfish ends.

The trials and tribulations of running stagecoach or freight lines, or of getting a contract to supply horses to

novel note. The film was pleasantly straightforward in its pitting of the forces of good against those of Western skulduggery, and in the final reel Bob bests the chief villain in the traditional fistic set-to. But seconds before the climactic clinch and "End" title, he springs the bombshell: the man he had just brought to book was, in addition to his other crimes, the man who had killed his father!

During the mid-thirties, there was also a curious but very entertaining rash of movies about the *making* of Westerns; Charles Starrett as a pampered Western star not allowed to ride a horse in *The Cowboy Star,* Gene Autry and Buck Jones as stuntmen doubles in *The Big Show* and *Hollywood Roundup* respectively, Richard Dix as a washed-up cowboy star who makes a comeback in *It Happened in Hollywood,* George O'Brien as a Western star accidentally involved in a real range war in *Hollywood Cowboy,* and later on, Gene Autry again as a double who rises to stardom, in *Shooting High.* There were others, all of them entertaining, off-beat, and often far more accurate in their depiction of working Hollywood than many much bigger productions. In the mid-forties there was a brief resurgence of this cycle, but on a less interesting level: Republic made a number of movies, *Bells of Rosarita* being the most typical, in

ences at least, the only respectable way to end any Western. When a Western introduced its fight early in the proceedings the rules seemed to have been broken, and the climax, no matter how exciting or spectacular in a non-fistic manner, seemed to be sadly lacking. If a Western was generous enough to have two fights, then it was considered a classic; if it had no fisticuffs at all, then it was beneath contempt and provoked loud boos. Considering how well-known these basic requirements were, it is surprising how often the cheaper Hollywood Western producers, outfits like Crescent and Puritan, flaunted the public's expectations by constantly delivering Westerns with no action at all. In the forties, as Westerns became more and more mass-produced, there

THE OFT-FILMED TALE: Pedro Armendariz, Harry Carey, Jr., and John Wayne in *Three Godfathers* (MGM, 1948)

which all of its currently active Western stars played themselves and left their studio in the lurch while they went to help Roy Rogers in his perennial battle against Grant Withers and Roy Barcroft!

Within the framework of these plot-lines, the action itself was often allotted certain specific uses. The runaway stagecoach or wagon was, for example, a perfect way for boy to meet girl. And, initially, the big fight between hero and villain (preferably after a horseback chase, although an on-foot encounter in the saloon was almost as acceptable) was considered, by juvenile audi-

was little to complain about in the action department. They were literally *all* fights and chases. At the PRC studios, Buster Crabbe only had to saunter into a saloon and Charles King would remark, "Stranger, I don't like your face," instantly provoking a vigorous if somewhat unconvincing fight.

It is only these latter-day, poverty-row Westerns that justify in any way the dismissal of the "B" Western as just a collection of clichés. The standardization of plot-lines had, of course, been growing slowly throughout the thirties, as more "B" Westerns were made, and as pro-

9

DOC HOLLIDAY'S WOMEN: Cesar Romero and Nancy Kelly in *Frontier Marshall* (Fox, 1939)

duction costs rose, making it imperative that they all be made more quickly and more economically. This increase in haste can also be seen in the carelessness with which titles were selected. In the silent period, most Westerns had titles directly applicable to their plot content. As the thirties arrived, there was a definite increase in the number of ambiguous titles: *Riders of the Rockies, Gunsmoke Trail, Phantom Ranger, West of the Pecos*. None of these titles had any direct relationship to the films they graced, but on the other hand, they weren't exactly unrelated either. The musical Westerns provided further leeway: *Sierra Sue, Ridin' Down the Canyon* and *In Old Monterey* (which was ultramodern and went nowhere *near* Monterey!) were not backed up by any characters, action or locations in their respective movies, but those title songs were sung somewhere along the way. Many Westerns of the forties had even more nebulous connections with their titles. *Covered Wagon Days* implied a historically-oriented tale of pioneer days, but it dealt with a goldmine and claim-

jumpers, with nary a covered wagon in sight. Zorro was never once referred to, let alone seen, in *Zorro's Black Whip,* Billy was likewise invisible in *Captive of Billy the Kid,* and *The Phantom Plainsmen* seems to be even more a case of pinning the tail on the donkey.

Oddly enough one rather spectacular cliché—far more remarkable than any number of "They went thattaway" utterances—was born in the "B" Western of the thirties, and stayed with it until its death in 1954. The heroine was, almost without exception, a biological freak—the offspring of but a single (male) parent. Western leading ladies never had mothers. Occasionally, when hard-pressed, a sympathetic father might utter, "Oh, if only your mother were alive . . . ," but that cursory nod to maternity apart, the mother was literally obliterated from the West. The reasons, of course, were economic, not genetic. A mother could never perform a useful function in a Western. Father could be robbed or cheated, used as a lever to force his daughter into marriage, or killed off, thus leaving the heroine entirely

10

dependent on the hero. Even a little brother or sister could be of some value; they could be kidnapped by the villain (as in *Moonlight on the Prairie*) or better still they might be crippled (as in *Heart of the Rockies* and *Arizona Badman*) and subject to frequent beatings by an evil stepfather, thus paving the way for intervention by the hero. But the mother could perform no such useful function. She couldn't even have babies, since pregnancies were unheard of in "B" Westerns and any babies that were seen were either survivors of Indian attacks, or orphans suddenly dumped in the hero's lap. Mothers couldn't be killed off, either, since that might be emotionally upsetting to the small fry. In other words, she was totally useless, eating up $200 of character actress money that could be better employed paying a stuntman for a horse fall. So the mother of the heroine remained a non-existent figure in the small-budget Westerns, rearing her unnecessary head only once, in Ken

DOC HOLLIDAY'S WOMEN: Kirk Douglas and Jo Van Fleet in *Gunfight at the OK Corral* (Paramount, 1956)

Maynard's *Heir to Trouble*. But then Maynard was always an unpredictable and innovational Western practitioner who could be counted on to come up with the unusual. It was television that restored Mother to her throne in the Western, and did so with a vengeance. Realizing that it is mother who buys the cereals and other goodies that the commercials bombard her offspring with, television couldn't afford to slight her. Far from just re-establishing her within the family as a figure that TV-watching moms could identify with, television put her on a pedestal, typified best by Barbara Stanwyck as an aggressive, entirely self-reliant head of a pioneering family in the *Big Valley* series.

Certainly the Western over its seventy-year history—and especially in the last forty of those years—has clung rigorously to a well-tried set of characters, story-lines and situations. But perhaps this is tradition rather than cliché. After all, if we apply the same standards to the seasons of the year, spring is very definitely a cliché. It comes along relentlessly at the same time every year, always without change, the same old re-vitalized fresh air, the same old colors in the countryside, the same old flowers. We neither want nor expect change, and love it for the same reasons that most of us love the Western—for its beauty, simplicity, and invigorating qualities. The perennial popularity of the Western, over and above specific box-office cycles, can perhaps be ascribed to the fact that it represents a way of life that has become a legend but is still sufficiently close to our own time for us to know that it *was* a reality. As time passes, our

THE FIGHT: John Wayne and Montgomery Clift in *Red River* (United Artists, 1948)

knowledge of the hardships of those days fades, and the good things stand out in greater contrast. Hemmed in as we are on all sides—involvement in wars, strikes, racial and social controversy, travel restrictions, bureaucracy, taxes, a countryside littered with beer cans and advertising billboards, city air polluted by chemicals and smog—it is reassuring and revitalizing to look back to a period less than a hundred years ago when a man could breathe free, clean air, go where he wanted, do as he pleased, and—for a few years at least, and if he were strong enough—be the sole master of his own destiny. We know those days can never come again, but we can steal them back, briefly, through the Western.

THE FIGHT: Guy Madison and Rory Calhoun in *Massacre River* (Allied Artists, 1949)

THE BEGINNINGS – AND BRONCHO BILLY

The Western movie, cashing in on the enormous popularity of the dime novel (itself glamorizing and exaggerating the Western frontier life that was rapidly disappearing but was still far from being ancient history), came into being even before there were theatre screens on which to show it. The first movies, often barely a minute in length and designed to be shown in the Mutoscope parlors, where only one person could view them at a time, cranking a handle as he looked into the peepshow machine, immediately recognized public interest in the West, and catered to it. Although the word had not been coined yet, many of these short vignettes were documentaries—scenes of cattle roundups or of the fast-vanishing buffalo herds grazing on the plains—and as such were, and are, an invaluable record of a changing America. Still others, while devoid of plots or acting, staged reconstructions of "typical" Western incidents: a stagecoach holdup or Indians scalping their victims. Buffalo Bill Cody was recorded on film; the Edison Company made a brief little tableau which they called *Cripple Creek Bar-room,* showing well-dressed, top-hatted Western dandies (gamblers presumably) lounging in the rough-and-ready bar, presided over by an apparently Indian female barkeeper. All of this was before the year 1900.

The big turning point came in 1903 with the Edison Company's *The Great Train Robbery,* filmed in New Jersey and directed by Edwin S. Porter. In view of the many Western vignettes that had preceded it, it was hardly, as has been claimed, the "first Western." Nor was it "the first story film," an even more exaggerated and frequently repeated claim. But it undoubtedly was the first Western with recognizable form; it established the essential formula of crime, pursuit, showdown and justice, and within its ten-minute running span it included, in addition to the train robbery itself, elements of fisticuffs, horseback pursuit and gunplay, along with suggestions of small child appeal, and probably the first introduction of that cliché-to-be, the saloon bullies forcing the dude into a dance. (In later years such a sequence was a useful contrivance to provoke a saloon fracas between the cavalier-hero and the bullying villain.) *The Great Train Robbery* was a remarkably sophisticated film for 1903, keeping briskly on the move and using its New Jersey locations intelligently, despite the too-Eastern and too-modern telegraph lines that paralleled the railroad track. There was interesting use of double-exposure and a neat bit of jump-cutting when

a dummy is substituted for one of the trainmen, and thrown off the engine after a fight scene.

Most of all however, the film benefitted from a primitive but effective form of editing, with intercutting between the opposing factions, and a good sense of storytelling and suspense. Porter, who directed and photographed, alas, didn't recognize the tremendous grammatical device he had stumbled onto. His film was put together that way because it seemed the logical way to tell a story, but many of his later films, including such post-1913 full-length features as *The Count of Monte Cristo,* were if anything a retrogression from *The Great Train Robbery* and had less innate cinema sense. Porter missed the opportunity to become the father of the *art* of cinema, but he did create the first American movie milestone. *The Great Train Robbery* was a huge commercial success and prompted not so much sequels and extensions as outright imitations. In those days of lax copyright protection (films were so new an entity that they were still copyrighted as photographs rather than

Cripple Creek Barroom, directed by W. K. L. Dickson for the Edison Company in 1898

Edwin S. Porter's
The Great Train Robbery
(1903): the shootout

motion pictures) it was all too easy for film pirates to make "dupe" negatives of completed pictures and sell them as their own, or at least inject key scenes into their own films. The Lubin Company of Philadelphia even went so far as to remake *The Great Train Robbery* scene for scene, with only an occasional detail—a different calendar for example—to show that it was *not* the identical film! Imitations and plagiarisms of *The Great Train Robbery* were legion, and a year or two later the Edison Company themselves made a parody of it, called *The Little Train Robbery*.

Despite the enormous popularity of the train robbery films (train robberies were still not uncommon, so the films had topicality as well as excitement), the growth of the Western was slow. Gradually, formulas began to evolve, the group of heroes and badmen giving way to individual good guys and bad guys. 1906's *A Race for Millions,* despite mixing rather obvious studio painted sets with genuine exteriors, had a solid little claim-jumping plot, an exciting auto *vs.* train chase (already Westerns were beginning to anticipate the Tom Mix and Roy Rogers streamlining by incorporating essentially modern ingredients into their plots), and a climax of the tra-

ditional *High Noon* man-to-man duel in the deserted main street. Already, too, the villain was moustachioed, black-hatted—and drank. Drinking not only lost him audience sympathy, but helped to explain why an experienced killer and gunman should be beaten to the draw by a comparatively innocent hero—a ploy that worked just as unobtrusively and effectively thirty-three years later in the climax of John Ford's *Stagecoach*. *A Race for Millions* was a big step forward in the evolution of the Western, but some key ingredients were still missing. All Westerns still ran for twelve minutes or less, limiting them to simple story-lines, and most of them were made in the East, in New York and New Jersey. There were still enough rugged locations, particularly in upstate New York, for the exteriors to double reasonably well for the real West, though occasionally a placid New Jersey stream didn't entirely live up to the "raging torrent" that a subtitle described it as. Physical action was still limited to fairly mild horseback cantering and brief, unconvincing wrestling. The profession of stuntman had yet to be born, and nobody knew yet how to stage spectacular horse-falls or no-holds-barred fistic battles, least of all the actors, many of them

16

recruited from the stage or the director's roster of family and friends. The acting—one might more accurately say "posing"—was stiff and unsubtle and the costuming a weird mixture of the actors' own Eastern wardrobes, decked out with ten-gallon hats, sheep-wool chaps, sheriff's badges, and other such essentials as could be borrowed, rented or made. The early Eastern Westerns certainly had a far from authentic look to them, and oddly enough, Westerns already being made in France (more rugged, with emphasis on violence, sudden death, lynchings) had much more genuine flavor to them, and more convincing locales and costuming. Audiences were more gullible and less critical then, however, and the shortcomings of the Eastern-filmed Westerns seemed not to worry them. That authenticity of costume, locale and plot was not in itself an essential to winning public appeal was proven by a most peculiar little Western of 1908 entitled *The Bank Robbery*. Produced by the Oklahoma Mutoscene Company, it was filmed entirely on location in and around Cache, Oklahoma. Its plot vaguely paralleled *The Great Train Robbery*, although it attempted to win a little sympathy for the outlaws by showing their concern for a wounded comrade, in putting their escape in jeopardy by stopping to care for him. The dusty little Oklahoma town, with the bank as its

focal point, was obviously the real thing, and at two reels the film was the longest Western yet made. Its "director" was famed frontier lawman William M. Tilghman (later a good friend and advisor to William S. Hart) and its cast included train robber Al Jennings, only recently out of jail. Tilghman undoubtedly was an efficient and fearless frontier marshal, but it is fortunate indeed that he never had to make his living as a movie director. Not only did he lack knowledge of even the rudiments of technique—some of the camera panning is so appallingly inept that once, when the outlaws race out of town, the camera never does catch up with more than a glimpse of the flying tail of the *last* horse—but he had no idea of showmanship either. One would have thought that with a "celebrity" like Al Jennings to work with, some attempt would have been made to spotlight him, either by making him the leader of the outlaws or by giving him a key scene or bit of "business." But there is not even a medium shot to give audiences the chance to recognize Jennings; he is merely one of the gang, photographed almost entirely in long shot throughout, and if one were not familiar with Jennings' face and small stature from his later starring Westerns, one wouldn't be able to pick him out from the crowd.

Fortunately, something happened in 1908 to weld the

Lubin's 1904 scene-by-scene copy of *The Great Train Robbery*

plots of the Eastern Westerns like *The Sheriff's Love* with the geographic authenticity of *The Bank Robbery,* and to add one vital ingredient. G. M. Anderson, a beefy former photographer's model with aspirations to acting and directing, had played several small parts in *The Great Train Robbery,* and in the intervening years had tried his hand at several other Westerns, none of them markedly successful. Then, without any inkling of the fantastic impact it would have, he made a short Western entitled *Broncho Billy and the Baby.* Because nobody else was currently available, he played the lead himself. Its title, and the story itself, came from a published Peter B. Kyne story. Anderson neglected the niceties of acquiring legal screen adaptation rights, and was soon visited by Kyne—who liked the film well enough to waive legal action, while at the same time making it clear that Anderson would have to be paid for any further adaptations of his work. The story was a pleasing mixture of action and sentiment, with a "good badman" hero who gives up his chance of freedom to aid a stricken child, and the film was an instant success. The reasons were not hard to discover, since the main departure from all previous Westerns was in its concentration on a colorful "hero"—a man who was rugged and a law unto himself,

but also possessed the nobility and courage of the Arthurian knights. Since the character had been tagged Broncho Billy, the name stuck, and Anderson became Broncho Billy Anderson in hundreds of one- and two-reel Westerns.

Up until this point, Anderson had considered himself more of a director and an executive than a star, and he was a partner in the Chicago-based Essanay Studio. Now, working out of Niles in California, he would devote himself almost exclusively to Broncho Billy. That he was not an especially handsome man hardly mattered (in fact, he resembled movie villain Fred Kohler more than he did standard leading-man types), since this early there was no star system. And as the first Western hero he was in any event creating precedents, not breaking them. He was a bad rider but learned quickly, and even managed a stunt or two as time went by. He was big and brawny, well able to look after himself in the fight scenes. He became quite adept at rope twirling. His bulky frame, paw-like hands and rough-hewn face even became advantages in his evolving characterization, enabling him to win laughs and audience sympathy with his clumsiness and lack of self-confidence in dealing with the ladies. The sheepish grin and the awkward fumbling

A Race for Millions (Edison, 1906), climaxed by a *High Noon*-type shootout

Early French Westerns:
The Hanging at Jefferson City
The Cowboy Kid

THE MOVING PICTURE WORLD

G. MÉLIÈS

DANNY TO THE RESCUE

THE COWBOY KID

A Photo-play which appeals to every lover of Western Life, showing the exploits of the eight year old "Danny," the youngest cowboy in the world. He alone discovered the revengeful plot to entrap his sister's fiance and by means of torture force him to acknowledge himself a thief and oust him from the country. With his sister's aid he released the artist and by his splendid riding brought the cowboys to the rescue whereby the gang of horse thieves who had so long terrorized the vicinity were finally tracked and all captured.

APPROX. 1000 FT.   G. MELIÈS, 204 EAST 38th St., NEW YORK CITY   7-6-12

with his hat when confronted by the heroine—a standard bit of business for every cowboy from Ken Maynard to John Wayne—was born in the Broncho Billy Westerns.

The Broncho Billy films were sure-fire audience pleasers, and while Anderson had none of the intense dedication to either art or the depiction of the true West that was to mark William S. Hart's work, he was a good showman and he learned quickly. His Westerns had strong little plots, and doubtless many of the standard "B" Western stories were first introduced to the screen by Anderson. Anderson's California locations gave his films a tremendous scenic advantage over the cowboy stories still being made in the East, and moreover they improved in quality, steadily and consistently. Relatively few of his films survive today, but those that do still have a great deal of vitality, charm, and often quite surprising production values. Even today, it's easy to understand his enormous appeal. Tom Mix came into movies with the Selig Company while Anderson was still at the peak of his popularity, and made but little initial impression. Later, of course, Mix would become the biggest Western star of them all. Anderson's popularity waned in 1914, when William S. Hart came to the screen with a subtler characterization, bigger budgets, and genuinely adult stories. Broncho Billy knew that he couldn't really compete, but he did go out with a flourish, making the transition to features and also, near the end of his career, producing some of his best and most polished shorts. One of these, *Shooting Mad,* is a

Broncho Billy's Christmas Dinner (Essanay, 1911)

Broncho Billy's Oath (Essanay, 1913)

Broncho Billy being interviewed on film in 1957: (left to right) actor John Griggs, historian Gerald D. McDonald, Anderson, cameraman Don Malkames, and William K. Everson.

Broncho Billy Anderson

21

kind of apotheosis of all the Broncho Billys, though its very last shot, a genial plagiarism from Chaplin's *Easy Street,* suggests that its approach was at least partially tongue-in-cheek. Still in circulation and frequently exhibited by film societies, it may mislead film scholars into an exaggerated concept of Anderson's accomplishments, since an archival error has dated it as 1912 instead of the correct 1918. For 1912, it would be a remarkable film indeed!

After 1920, with Hart at his prime, Tom Mix rapidly overtaking him, and any number of new Western stars on the way, Anderson returned briefly to producing (with a series of Stan Laurel comedies) and then drifted out of movies entirely. He came into the limelight again in the late fifties, when he was rediscovered and pressed into service as a guest star in a brace of TV documentaries on the Western. And in 1965 he joined other Western old-timers at the Paramount studio to play a character cameo in his first sound, color and wide-screen Western, *The Bounty Killer*. Exactly sixty-two years after his first appearance in a Western saloon in *The Great Train Robbery,* he was sitting in a Western saloon again—not spry enough to re-do his spirited dance, but with those eagle eyes as alert as ever, as though aware that everything that was taking place before the camera had been pioneered in his Broncho Billy Westerns six decades earlier. He has never been bitter at the relatively brief tenure of his years of movie fame; after all he had been *in The Great Train Robbery,* and he had single-handedly established the Western Star and set up the basic formula of the series-Western. The Broncho Billys were the bedrock on which William S. Hart, Tom Mix, D. W. Griffith, Thomas Ince, and John Ford would now build the art of the Western.

PIONEERS OF THE ART: D.W. GRIFFITH AND THOMAS H. INCE

Although their tremendous contributions to the development of the film as a whole far transcend their importance to the Western, nevertheless the Western film in its early, formative days owed a huge debt to David Wark Griffith and Thomas H. Ince.

Both came to films at approximately the same time and both made their most important contributions to film in the years 1908-1913. Admittedly, Griffith's great masterpieces came later, but they wouldn't have been possible without the "language" of film that he evolved in those earlier years and which has been absorbed by every film-maker since. Ince's importance was even more indisputably restricted to those early years, since his creative career dwindled rapidly after 1916, even

though he remained active and prolific until his death in the mid-twenties.

The two men complemented one another rather nicely. Griffith was wholly devoted to the art of film and to developing new and dynamic means of story-telling. He worked creatively and intuitively and had a poor head for business organization. His personal drive and enthusiasm could help raise financing for production, but once his films were made, his lack of experience in marketing prevented their making money for him, although others might profit enormously from them. In any case, once a film was finished, he was much more concerned with his next project. Ince, conversely, though initially a director too, soon became much more valuable as a production supervisor, establishing methods of organizing film-making on the most economical assembly-line basis possible. He supervised other directors, rewrote scenarios, insisted on super-detailed scripts that gave the director every kind of assistance by outlining mood, describing the sets or locations, explaining how certain effects could be achieved at minimum cost, giving the cameraman tips as to the style of lighting and the color tints to be used, and providing complete dialogue for all of the characters so that the actors would really understand their roles, even though the films were silent, and all of the dialogue would ultimately have to be condensed to a few subtitles. Griffith, on the other hand, used no scripts at all—a practice he followed even

David W. Griffith

in his huge historical spectacles—working entirely by instinct and keeping not only complicated plot-lines but his even more complicated editing plans in his head. Their individual methods worked well for both film-makers; a Griffith film was always recognizably a Griffith film and an Ince film always had the Ince stamp on it—quite literally, since Ince was rather a vain man and loved to see his name on the credits of his films as often as possible. It was even printed on the ends of reels—footage never intended to be projected and there merely for identification purposes! Both approaches to film-making were extreme, but they produced far greater results than the compromise methods employed by other studios. The Edison Company, for example, utilized scripts that were literally no more than lists of shots with the barest of details. They offered no help to an unimaginative director and no stimulus to a talented one. Actually, the directorial talent at Edison seemed to be on a par with the writing talent; apart from the early pioneering works of Edwin S. Porter, almost everything that emerged from the Edison Studios was stodgy and at least five years behind the times in terms of technique.

Both Griffith and Ince made a great number of one- and two-reel Westerns. Ince made them because he had established standing sets of Western towns and ranches, and maintained a permanent troupe of cowboys, Indians and trick riders, with attendant wagons, horses, cattle, buffalo and other livestock. Griffith made Westerns because they provided him with a perfect framework on which to hang stories of action and suspense. Although he made many potboilers—simple little romances and dramas—his important work fell into one of two categories. On the one hand, he was making films that had something of cultural or social importance to *say:* adaptations of literary classics or comments on current political or social attitudes. On the other, he was turning out what could loosely be termed "chase" films—thrillers, train robbery films, modern piracy on the high seas, gangster stories, and most of all, Westerns. Most of these films had the simplest of story-lines: a few deft scenes to establish period and milieu and then right into a single basic situation which would be milked for suspense and action. The Western, with its already standard situation of the "good" guys besieged by villains or Indians, and the climactic race to the rescue, provided Griffith with the perfect background for his experiments in film "grammar." Griffith obviously loved the chase, for the excitement it created and he continued to use it, constantly developing and polishing, right through his career. But in these early Westerns he used it not just for its own inherent thrill, but also as a way of involving audiences emotionally in his films, of making them par-

Thomas H. Ince and his Indian star
William Eagleshirt

Griffith as an actor in Edwin S. Porter's
Rescued from an Eagle's Nest (Edison, 1907)

Griffith's *Ramona* (Biograph, 1910)

Griffith's *The Last Drop of Water* (Biograph, 1911)

ticipants rather than spectators. Just how advanced Griffith was in his ideas, and how little they were understood by his contemporaries, can be clearly indicated by a comparison of two Westerns almost identical in plot content but poles apart in terms of excitement and style—the Edison Company's *The Corporal's Daughter* of 1915 and Griffith's *Fighting Blood* of 1911.

The Corporal's Daughter, not considered a bad film in its day, merely an average but quite acceptable product, is almost an object lesson in how to take foolproof material and even in the short running time of ten minutes make it seem dull and overlong. The characters are all flung on the screen without any kind of establishing scenes; titles tell us who they are and explain their relationships to other characters, and that is all. There are no seemingly extraneous "bits of business" to humanize them, no closeups of their faces to give us any idea of what their emotions are. Even the little suspense that the story has is minimized by titles that tell us beforehand what is going to happen. Menacing Indians ride into static camera set-ups in long shot and stop just in front of the camera to perform their essential bit of action. A title informs us that the gallant band of cavalrymen is hopelessly besieged by Indians and fight-

Edison's *The Corporal's Daughter* (1915) with New Jersey sewer well in evidence

Griffith's *Goddess of Sagebrush Gulch* (Biograph 1912) with Blanche Sweet

ing back bravely, yet the accompanying action shows us a dozen or more soldiers, strategically positioned high on a hill with plenty of rocks for cover, shooting down at the Indians, of whom we see only two or three. When the relief force is sent to the rescue, they gallop out of a fort which is a reasonable enough set, but which loses in conviction when we see that it is built back from a main highway, with a gaping sewer prominent in center-screen. (A minor shift of the camera could have avoided it with ease.) As for the rescue: the cavalry suddenly appears on the scene without any attempt at cross-cutting to build tension and excitement and the film finishes abruptly with the standard hero-heroine embrace. There is no neat little comic or human touch to round it out.

Looking at this very primitive Western today, it is difficult indeed to believe that Griffith's far more sophisticated *Fighting Blood* came a full four years earlier. Griffith instantly wins audience sympathy by showing us a likeable family of pioneers, with a large contingent of children, eking out a hard existence. The father is a Civil War veteran and trains his children in military drill. In a few deft scenes, Griffith sketches in their innate patriotism, establishes one child as mischievous, the

oldest son as being in love and as something of a rebel against parental authority.

Well within the first third of this ten-minute film, separate sub-plots have evolved. The Sioux are on the war-path. The son has fallen out with his father, gone to visit his girl, become involved in some skirmishing with the Indians, and decided to get help. At one point, as the hero (Bobby Harron) tries to mount his horse to go for help, the horse, scared, shies away. Probably having had no time (or excess film) to re-shoot the scene, Griffith just uses as much of it as he can, cuts away to something else, and then returns to find the hero safely on his horse—a bit of elementary editing that obviously never occurred to the Edison director confronted with that sewer! From here the film builds constantly in its tension and in the sheer size of its action, cutting from the hero racing for help (followed by three Indians whom he engages in a running horseback duel) to the settlers fighting off the Indians.

And even in these tremendously well-staged action scenes, Griffith never forgets to engage audience sympathy: two of the children cower under the bed, as excited as they are frightened; an older girl pantomimes that she can't shoot the guns because the noise hurts

Kate Bruce and
Lillian Gish in Griffith's
*The Battle of Elderbush
Gulch* (Biograph, 1913)

her ears, but she'll do her bit by loading them for the others. The cabin is set afire, and water to control it is getting low. The hero meanwhile has reached a large body of cavalry, which rushes to the rescue. Imaginative camera placement here manages to suggest literally hundreds of riders by having the audience first see a long line of riders racing to the right of the screen at a great distance away, and then, a few moments later, the apparent front rank of that line gallops into the forefront of the frame. This was a shot that Griffith repeated exactly in his 1924 epic, *America*. Now Griffith cuts back more and more between the battle and the rescue troop, and finally, when the cavalry races on to the scene, he has his camera high atop a hill, creating a vast panorama which takes in the cabin, the encircling Indians, and the rescuing cavalry in extreme yet crystal-clear long shots. To round off his tale, Griffith stages an emotional reunion between father and son, and for a final fillip, has the now beaming children emerge from under the bed on to a floor realistically covered with spent cartridges. *Fighting Blood* was quite possibly the best directed and edited film of 1911, yet the fact that the similarly-plotted but totally styleless *The Corporal's*

Daughter was still considered acceptable in 1915 shows not only how advanced Griffith's methods were, but also how little they were understood by his competitors. Of course, *The Birth of a Nation,* also in 1915, proved that his methods were not only artistically brilliant but commercially sound, and *then* directors were only too willing to try to copy his innovational style.

Griffith continued to make many outstanding one- and two-reel Westerns for Biograph, almost all of them made in Hollywood, where the rugged scenery gave them a tremendous scenic advantage over their Eastern counterparts. From simple little dramas like *Friends, The Goddess of Sagebrush Gulch,* and *Broken Ways,* he progressed to spectacular films on epic themes: *The Last Drop of Water* (a 1911 precursor to *The Covered Wagon*), *The Battle of Elderbush Gulch* (Lillian Gish and Mae Marsh in a superb action film, with savage massacre scenes and brilliantly constructed and edited battle scenes), and perhaps best of all, *The Massacre,* a stark, yet poetic film, based very loosely on the Custer massacre and decidedly sympathetic to the Indian point of view. As were many of the later Griffith films, it was also a parable on the futility of war. The "massacre"

War on the Plains (Ince, 1912)

Ethel Grandin in scenes from *Blazing the Trail* (Ince, 1912)

The Invaders (Ince, 1912)

The Deserter (Ince, 1912) with Francis Ford (John's brother)

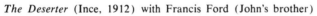

of the title is not absolute. One by one the settlers fall, gambler and priest dying side by side. When the rescue troop arrives on the scene of carnage, it finds only the dead—until a hand waves feebly from beneath a pile of corpses. The heroine and her baby whom she is clutching to her breast are the sole survivors. Although Griffith and Ince both made Westerns in which the Indians were the standard, unmotivated villains, convenient mass targets in the battle scenes, they also made a great many that were sympathetic to the Indian and critical of the whites' actual (though indirect) policy of extermination. Films like Ince's *The Indian Massacre* were meticulous

The Battle of the Redmen (Ince, 1912)

The Indian Massacre
(Ince, 1912)
with Ann Little,
Francis Ford

not only in documenting the Indian's way of life, but in establishing him as a human being of nobility and recognizable emotions. *The Indian Massacre* was one of the best of these films, presenting both sides of the picture, stressing the problems and courage of the white settlers, but emphasizing most of all the tragedy of the relentless extermination of the Indian. Its closing scene—a silhouette of an Indian woman praying beneath the wood-frame burial pyre of her dead child—was as beautifully composed and photographed as anything in later John Ford films.

Stories of the American Indian were a dominant motif in the early Westerns, and especially those of Griffith and Ince. In fact, James Fenimore Cooper was much more of an influence on the Western movie at this time than Zane Grey. Many films eschewed the Indian-white conflict entirely to deal with themes of wholly Indian content—simple romances like *Little Dove's Romance,* or melodramas such as Griffith's *A Squaw's Love,* with Mabel Normand engaged in some stunt leaps and underwater swimming in a story of intertribal intrigue. Direct adaptations of Fenimore Cooper stories *(The Deerslayer, Leatherstocking)* were very popular too, though not strictly Westerns since geographically they were set

along the Eastern seaboard and for the most part were shot in New York or New Jersey. And already in this period the movies had exploited the theme of the "college" Indian returning, educated, to his people, only to be rejected by them and yet unable to return to the white man's cities. Thomas Ince tended to concentrate rather more on the Indian films than did Griffith for two very good reasons. One was that he had a considerable investment in his Indian riders, tepees, buffalo and other livestock, and liked to use them as frequently as possible. Another was that he was far more of a "story" man than Griffith, and the American Indian offered a wealth of material. To Griffith, technique was everything. His "stories" were usually little more than situations. Ince, on the other hand, was never very strong on technique. There is superb staging in his films, realistic detail, expert and often spectacular mass action scenes, and fine camerawork. But in terms of directorial finesse and editing, he ran a very second best to Griffith. However, his stories were strong in the extreme, running to a multiplicity of characters and presenting themes of moral regeneration and self-sacrifice. The movies were still not considered "respectable" in many quarters, and they constantly sought to justify themselves by teaching

Desert Gold
(Ince, 1914)
with Clara Williams,
Frank Borzage,
Bob Kortman

valuable "moral lessons" with their entertainment. Ince did more than his share along these lines, and his films were full of ministers or evangelical "good badmen" who conquered or won over the lawless elements and cowards who found themselves. The clear distinction between good and evil was depicted by pitting church against saloon in such short early Westerns as *Past Redemption.*

Moral retribution in Ince Westerns was unusually severe. The heroine of *The Woman* marries bigamously only to raise money for her desperately ill husband, this after having taken a bad fall in the Cherokee Strip landrush (a very creditably staged sequence) in an effort to gain land in a warm climate where he might recover. After her first husband dies, she feels that she has betrayed both him and her current husband. The only solution, suicide. Ann Little, the heroine of *Past Redemption,* formerly sold firewater to the Indians and had shot down a cavalryman or two. She was thoroughly "saved" by the church, but when the minister fell in love with her, she was so obviously unworthy that the only way out was for her to trek across the desert, and die of thirst. (The mortality rate in Ince's Civil War films was even higher!) While seen individually these tragic Ince Westerns seem genuinely dramatic, seen as a group the rather pointless contrivance of so much of the tragedy emerges instead as a kind of gimmick: Ince used the shock ending of tragedy just as Griffith used the excitement of the chase. The stress on unhappy endings was certainly unconventional, but it was perhaps not quite as daring as it might seem today. The star system was still in its earliest stages, and in any case, prior to Charles Ray and William S. Hart, Ince had no stars of major importance. Thus audiences were not sufficiently familiar with such players as Francis Ford and Tom Chatterton to regard them as favorites or to be dismayed when they were suddenly killed off.

The majority of Ince's Westerns were either cowboy-Indian or cavalry-Indian affairs, often surprisingly elaborate in the scale of their action, and frequently, as in *The Invaders,* running to three reels in length instead of the customary two. His canny business sense told him that it was worth spending extra money on big battle and action scenes, since these could later be re-used and cut into other films with similar themes and players. He was thus the first producer to deliberately economize by using stock footage—something that became a fine art in the last days of the "B" Western, when eighty per cent of the action material would be stock lifted

33

A much later re-issue poster for Ince's 1912 *Custer's Last Fight*

Griffith's only feature-length Western: 1919's *Scarlet Days*, (Paramount) with Richard Barthelmess and Carol Dempster

Scarlet Days: Barthelmess and (center) George Fawcett

from earlier pictures. However, the polish and scope of Ince's original action footage can be attested to by the fact that it was still being used to pad out new pictures even into the 1950's.

In 1913 Griffith left Biograph to move out to Hollywood and the less restricting Reliance company. He had big plans, and the Western for him had served its purpose. Indeed, for the rest of his career, he would personally direct only one more Western, 1919's *Scarlet Days,* one of his least successful features. It was little more than one of his standard Biograph one-reel plots expanded to eight times that length, although with the traditional last-reel fight and race to the rescue to provide the expected climactic excitement.

Ince, on the other hand, though no longer a personal director, was on the threshold of accidentally making one of the greatest contributions of all to the future well-being of the Western film. For in 1914 he would introduce to movie audiences a veteran stage actor, William Surrey Hart. Hart had been associated with "classic" theatre, and especially Shakespeare for so long that to this day the legend persists that the "S" in his name stands for Shakespeare. Most stage players who were brought to the screen in the first days of full-length silent features failed badly, and after their initial novelty wore off, returned to the boards. The three most notable exceptions of the 1914-16 years were William S. Hart, John Barrymore, and Douglas Fairbanks. Hart was the first to make movies and to establish an international reputation through them. The French loved him, and dubbed him "Rio Jim." As the Westerns left the one- and two-reelers behind and moved into full features, they needed a guiding hand desperately—not just a gifted director or a colorful star. Bill Hart was the perfect example of the right man in the right place at precisely the right time.

WILLIAM S. HART

To many, William S. Hart is the embodiment of the "strong, silent" Western hero of the screen, a stereotyped if nostalgic figure, and no more. And admittedly, one's first introduction to Hart (depending, of course, on the film) often does tend to substantiate that impression. But how inaccurate it is, and what an injustice it does to a man who was not just a star but, together with John Ford, a major force in the shaping and development of the Western genre.

Hart was a mature man when he came to the movies in 1914, with long theatrical experience, primarily Shakespearean, behind him. The Western film, even that early, had sunk into disrepute. D. W. Griffith had abandoned his fine little Biograph Westerns to move into more ambitious features, and in any case he had never developed a single Western *star* with recognizable characteristics and costume that carried over from picture to picture. Rather, he used his regular roster of players—Charles West, Henry B. Walthall, Alfred Paget, Walter Miller, Lionel Barrymore and others—all of whom played Easterners, Westerners, Northerners and Southerners with fine impartiality. Only Harry Carey seemed to fit most naturally into Western roles, and of course as soon as he left Biograph he was to specialize in them. Tom Mix was still marking time in uninspired Selig shorts, and Broncho Billy, tremendously popular though he was, was producing the Easterner's concept of what the Western should be.

Although not quite the authentic plainsman that Hart, in later years, loved to pose as (through a sheer love of that pose, not out of a desire to deceive), Hart had spent much of his youth in the West. He had seen frontier gunfighting at first hand, knew the American Indian, and had a baby brother buried on the prairie. He genuinely loved the West, and when, quite unexpectedly, he found himself a star after his first film, he was determined to put the truth, the poetry, and the history of the West on film. With producer Thomas Ince's backing he did this, to a critical acclaim and popular success neither of them had dreamed of. A shrewd producer and somewhat of an opportunist, Ince later exploited Hart ruthlessly, and at one point such hostility existed between the two men that Hart refused to let his pinto pony Fritz (the first of many movie horses to have his own huge fan following) appear in any of the movies from which Ince would profit. Hart even took big trade-paper advertisements to announce Fritz's "retirement"—and later on, when he had left Ince, his "comeback." But regardless of the business and personal differences between the men, Ince deserves a great deal of credit for giving Hart his first opportunity, and for having the foresight to recognize Hart's potential and give him a free hand with his films.

Rapidly graduating from one-reelers to features, Hart surrounded himself with a stock company of players, writers (C. Gardner Sullivan was the best, and was to remain a major screenwriter for many years), directors (Lambert Hillyer, Reginald Barker) and cameramen, but he was the guiding spirit behind all his films and frequently the actual, not just the nominal, director. Because Hart's films were always so dominated by his personality as an actor, his skill as a director has usually been either underrated or ignored entirely. In 1914-15, the art of direction was still relatively new. Griffith was supreme, most of the major directors of the silent era were still just apprentices, and there were only a handful of really accomplished directors on the next plateau below Griffith: Cecil B. DeMille, Maurice Tourneur, Herbert Brenon, Charles Chaplin, and Hart. And Hart certainly belongs in that illustrious company, even though his range was narrower than the others. His control of mob scenes was often superb, he managed to extract extremely subtle underplaying from his leading ladies, and while he wasn't one for showy technique, he understood the tools of film and when best to use them. He rarely moved his camera for example, but when he did, it was to a purpose—as in *The Return of Draw Egan*, when the camera tracks in front of him as he

On the Night Stage
(Triangle, 1914)
with William S. Hart
and Robert Edeson

Hell's Hinges (Triangle, 1916)

Hell's Hinges

strides resolutely from his sheriff's office for a street showdown with the villain. His films were raw, unglamorous, and gutsy, the costumes and livery trappings accurate, the ramshackle Western towns and their inhabitants like unretouched Matthew Brady photographs, the sense of dry heat ever-present (panchromatic filmstock, developed in the twenties, softened and glamorized the landscapes in later Westerns), and the clouds of dust everywhere. (This naturalistic quality vanished later when directors took to wetting down the ground so that the riding scenes would be cleaner and crisper.)

Hart's films were the first "adult" Westerns in the truest sense of that much distorted phrase. Hart knew the West, counted such lawmen as Wyatt Earp and Bat Masterson among his friends, and sincerely did his best to mingle poetry and realism in his films. His zeal did occasionally lead him astray; his sentimentality began to dominate his later films, and even honesty can become a cliché when it is presented via situations, characters and a style of subtitling that are repeated in almost every film. However, Hart's clichés were very personal ones, so personal that they never became absorbed into the mainstream of Western film clichés. He loved his sister dearly, and a recurring theme in several of his movies called on him to avenge the death, seduction, or other

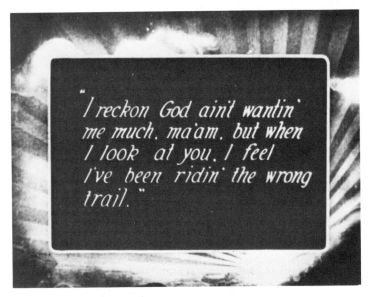

A typical C. Gardner Sullivan title:
Hell's Hinges

The Testing Block (Paramount, 1920) with Eva Novak

Three Word Brand (Paramount, 1921)

betrayal of a sister. To Hart, every woman was a lady, to be respected and protected with the chivalry of old. Thus his "good badman" character invariably reformed almost from the first glance of his leading lady. "One who is evil looking for the first time on that which is good" is how a subtitle in *Hell's Hinges* (1916) put it, to be followed shortly thereafter by: "I reckon God ain't wantin' me much, Ma'am, but when I look at you I feel I've been ridin' the wrong trail." Hart, a supreme sentimentalist, not only identified himself with his screen image, but cherished and revered all of his leading ladies, off-screen as well as on, to the extent of proposing marriage to most of them. (Only one of them, Winifred Westover, liked the idea. Hart, aghast, tried to back out, but she pursued him with grim determination. The marriage took place but was not a happy one, and they later divorced.)

Since Hart had an unerring eye for beauty and taste in his leading ladies (Bessie Love, Eva Novak, Jane Novak, Anna Q. Nilsson) his instantaneous conversions were often surprisingly convincing, really falling down only when the rather plain Clara Williams was his nemesis. "A different kind of smile, sweet, honest and trustful, and seeming to say 'How do you do, friend?'" was the masterfully creative subtitle that C. Gardner

Sullivan wrought to accompany a bland expression, excessive eye makeup and a hesitant twitch of the lips when Miss Williams first confronted badman Hart. As a change of pace (as in *The Testing Block,* where Hart played the leader of a gang of outlaws collected "by the broom that swept hell") Hart occasionally got roaring drunk, or thoroughly disillusioned with women (or both) and forced the heroine into marriage with him at gunpoint. Such ungentlemanly behavior always took place at the beginning of the film, however, allowing Hart ample time for remorse and self-sacrifice, and allowing the heroine equally ample time to fall genuinely in love with him and present him with a child.

On the whole, Hart's batting average was high. His early features were the best, and the tightest. He would spend roughly one month shooting a feature at a budget of $14,000, his own salary considerably less than $2,000. No wonder that Ince made a small fortune, and that Hart felt himself ill-used. Nevertheless, Hart's resentment never reflected itself in his films. He kept turning out Westerns—and an occasional non-Western—of quality and excitement. Sometimes, as in *Hell's Hinges,* a kind of Western *Sadie Thompson,* he included plot elements (the systematic seduction of a weak minister by the town trollop) that even today would be consid-

As Wild Bill Hickok (Paramount, 1923)

ered daring in a Western. Action was not necessarily a prime ingredient in the Hart Westerns, though he was a good rider and a rugged athlete who rarely used doubles in his fight scenes. But many of the films tended to be stronger on plot and characterization than on fast physical action. This hardly mattered in the 1914-18 years, when his formula was still relatively fresh, and when his films had such good plots and taut construction that interest never flagged. But after 1919, the originality began to fade, and the pace slackened. Hart, after all, was already forty-four when he made his first film; now his age began to be emphasized by plots which contained romantic liaisons with girls at least twenty years his junior. As if to stress Hart's he-man virility, they were never May-December romances, but always boy-girl romances, and Hart's sentimentality in these sub-plots began to dominate more and more of the footage. The films slowed down—at the very time when Tom Mix was in his ascendancy and had established a market for slick, streamlined, all-action movies. Hart had never liked action for its own sake, and apart from isolated highlight scenes—a horseback leap from a cliff or through a plate-glass window—his films are almost totally devoid of stuntwork. (In *Tumbleweeds* one shot of a runaway wagon approaching a gully was done by a trick glass-shot; another wagon crash was done in two shots with a cutaway in between; neither scene needed the services of a stuntman and neither scene was notably exciting.) He undoubtedly felt that elaborate stunts smelled of trickery; he'd settle for a lesser thrill but greater conviction. But in the wake of the Tom Mix Westerns (and Mix was to emphasize action, play down realism, and go out deliberately for small-child appeal), Hart's films seemed increasingly old-fashioned. Asked by his studio to move with the times, "modernize" his films, and restore their decreasing box-office returns, Hart refused. Grimly sticking to his principles, he was determined to make films *his* way or not at all. And to his credit, he faltered badly only once, with an absurd Western titled *Singer Jim McKee* that had a rambling, incoherent plot line, an excess of lugubrious sentimentality, and a total disregard for time and logic. Hart, already a veteran reformed outlaw, raises the baby of a fallen comrade to womanhood, ultimately marries her, serves time in jail, and returns to her and their child in what must conservatively have been his 110th year! Hart's other later Westerns, however, slower paced or not, were still good films, and they still carried the mark of his own integrity. His *Wild Bill Hickok* (prefaced by a title in which Hart apologized to his audience for looking more like Bill Hart than Bill Hickok) had two well-staged gun-fight highlights, and a reasonable, if

romanticized, respect for the historical facts, even bringing in an ignored (by Hollywood) period in Hickok's life when he was going blind and, for obvious reasons of self-preservation, had to conceal the fact.

Hart made his last film in 1925. It was his biggest, and his only genuine, epic, *Tumbleweeds*. Despite one minor concession to popular taste—Hart had a comic sidekick in Lucian Littlefield—and some protracted comedy and romantic interludes with the heroine, it was a fine film, worthy of being ranked with *The Covered Wagon* and *The Iron Horse* as a major Western epic. Directed by Hart and King Baggott, it had as its highlight a massively spectacular reconstruction of the Cherokee Strip landrush, which was not only splendidly staged and photographed but also edited with a precision and a mathematical rhythm worthy of Eisenstein. Later landrush sequences—for example, the two versions of *Cimarron*—borrowed a great deal from this, and while they were slicker, and *looked* bigger because of their utilization of panoramic long shots taken from high camera cranes, and action shots taken from camera trucks, they also looked like what they were: Hollywood reconstructions. Hart's version has the look of a contemporary newsreel, even to the retention of one or two awkward panning shots where the camera temporarily loses the rider it is following. Since Hart did all of his own hard riding even though he was now nearing the age of fifty-six, one could easily have forgiven him if he had pandered to his vanity a little and included some running inserts—riding closeups taken from a camera truck running parallel to, or in front of, his horse. But Hart had always been reluctant to use such a device for a galloping rider, undoubtedly feeling that it would too readily suggest the omnipresence of a camera crew. He would occasionally use running inserts of a stagecoach, but to spotlight his own riding skill he used them only once—in the horse-race climax of one of his best pictures, *The Narrow Trail*. Hart quite certainly knew exactly what he was doing in the staging and photography of his landrush sequence, and if the individual thrill is lost through the minimizing of stuntwork and camera fluidity, then the cumulative thrill more than makes up for it. The sequence comes to its close on a scene of sheer poetry: Hart, finally out in front, gallops his horse over the crest of a rise, and the camera, angled slightly above ground level, picks out for a few seconds one of the loveliest images any film has ever given us, a horse and rider, free of restraint and contact with the earth, apparently galloping through space.

Although mishandled by its distributors and not reaching anywhere near its full commercial potential, *Tumbleweeds* was both a critical and popular success

43

and vindicated Hart and his methods. Wisely, he didn't try to top it. And prophetically, he had included a scene early in the film wherein he, with a group of riders, reins in his horse on the top of a hill. He removes his hat, and looks off at the great cattle herds winding their way across the plains, evacuating the land that is soon to be thrown open to homesteaders. "Boys," he says, "It's the last of the West." *Tumbleweeds* was the last of the West for Hart too. He had no wish, nor need, to stay on making Westerns in the style that the studios wanted but that he personally despised. He retired to his Newhall ranch to write his autobiography (a vivid, if romanticized work) and books of equally vivid western fiction and poetry. When *Tumbleweeds* was reissued in 1939, to cash in on the great new Western cycle launched by *Stagecoach,* Hart faced the cameras once more to film a memorable ten-minute introduction to it. First as a story-teller, outlining the historic facts behind the opening up of the Cherokee Strip, and then as a moviemaker proud of his record, recalling the past with deep emotion and honest sentiment, and finally bidding farewell to his audience for the last time, Hart brought all

Wild Bill Hickok (Paramount, 1923)

44

Tumbleweeds (United Artists, 1925) with Barbara Bedford

of his long theatrical and Shakespearean experience to bear. His voice, rich, beautifully modulated, occasionally dangerously close to a sob, not only made this introductory speech one of the most poignant ever put on film, but made many people realize for the first time what a magnificent contribution Hart could have made to the sound film as a star, had he been younger, or as a character actor, had he been inclined.

Whether, in the long run, Hart's influence on the Western was as far-reaching as John Ford's or Tom Mix's is both debatable and unimportant. But quite certainly, in the context of his time (and Hart's career spanned a mere eleven years, as opposed to twenty-five years for Mix, and fifty for Ford), he made the major contribution, rescuing the Western from obscurity, gaining for it both artistic and commercial respect, and in Europe—and France especially—establishing the legend and myth of the American West on a level so far superior to that of the novel that such intellectuals as Jean Cocteau were instantly (and permanently) caught in its spell.

45

JOHN FORD:
A HALF-CENTURY OF HORSE OPERAS

In the long run, director John Ford has probably contributed more to the Western film than any other individual. Certainly he has made more Westerns than any other major director and has maintained a higher standard over the years than such other front-rank directors as Howard Hawks, Henry King, Henry Hathaway and Raoul Walsh, who admittedly never specialized in the Western, but did return to it frequently as a kind of aesthetic and commercial haven. Oddly enough, although he made close to sixty of them, Ford has always played down any great personal affection or talent for the Western. As recently as 1968, in an interview filmed for BBC Television, he stated that "none of my so-called better pictures were Westerns," and maintained that his main reason for making Westerns was that it enabled him to get away from Hollywood and into the open and to work with crews and players that were old friends.

However, Ford has always been notorious for his dislike of all interviewers and—a trait that has grown with old age and crotchety irascibility—for his tendency never to give a straight answer. Opinions and "facts" given to one interviewer are often directly contradicted by those given to another. Ford's dislike of the sham and artifice of so many pretentious directors is commendable, but he often goes to the other extreme, denying *any* qualities of art·in his films. "It's just a job of work, that's all . . . you do the best you can . . . like the man digging the ditch, who says 'I hope the ground is soft so that my pick digs deeper.'"

Stars and technicians who have worked with Ford confirm his easy-going attitude and his lack of deliberate striving after "art," yet Ford's films themselves more than refute his dismissal of them. As with no other American director, they all bear his recognizable signature. Whether his films were photographed by Joseph August, Arthur Miller or Gregg Toland, they all looked like Ford pictures. Familiar faces are scattered through all of them, a Ford stock company nurtured and built through the years. John Wayne made his first appearance in a Ford film with a sizeable bit role in 1928's *Hangman's House*.

The musical scores—with frequent recourse to "Red River Valley," whether the film is a Western or not—all *sound* like Ford scores. No matter how adept cameramen, players and composers were at knowing the kind of mood or result that Ford wanted, the consistent style of the finished pictures had to come from Ford himself. Although he did occasionally re-shoot scenes deemed unsatisfactory after a picture was officially completed,

this rarely happened. He always worked quickly and efficiently, and when the film was wrapped up, he looked forward to the next project instead of fussing with the mechanical laboratory polishing of the completed work. However, he left the studio personnel little option but to present the film as he had shot it; Ford turned in little excess footage—no alternate shots for tricky sequences or added closeups to boost the ego of a star. In a sense he edited his films in the camera. His virtues—a strong pictorial sense, vigorous action, honest sentiment, the ability to get away with a plot cliché and make it seem fresh and dramatic, the outstanding performances he got from players (John Wayne, Victor McLaglen, Wallace Ford) who were often weak under other directors—were as consistent as his weaknesses. These included a too-strong penchant for slapstick comedy, the professional Irishman's dislike of the British (expressed through many barbed and overdrawn British stereotypes), and a sloppiness in constructing what he considered unimportant sequences. The use of back projection, non-matching locales and cut-in closeups (as in John Wayne's first appearance in *Stagecoach*), and

Straight Shooting (Universal, 1917) with Harry Carey and Hoot Gibson

Harry Carey,
Ford's first big star

Straight Shooting: **A** favorite location

obvious studio "exteriors" marred many Ford Westerns. But to his credit, he never "cheated" in the big dramatic or action scenes. *Stagecoach* may be full of non-matching locales (the rugged Monument Valley locations in Utah intercut with scenes filmed in drab Chatsworth, just a few miles outside Hollywood) but once Ford sweeps into the magnificent chase across the salt flats, or follows Wayne through the streets of Lordsburg in the climax, there is never a hint of economy or production corner-cutting. Nor does Ford ever mind "breaking the rules" of orthodox film-making if the pictorial results justify it. Many times in the chase in *Stagecoach* there are abrupt changes in screen direction—the coach going right to left one moment, left to right the next—but the sequence is so superbly built that one hardly notices. One such particularly abrupt cut was made solely so that Ford could shoot directly into the sun and achieve a marvelous tracking shot of the coach speeding along through the dust and twilight.

Ford's films, put together, provide a surprisingly comprehensive survey of Americana and American history, ranging through the War of Independence, the Civil War and its aftermath, the opening up of the West, the decimation of the American Indian, immigration at the turn of the century, World War I, prohibition and the gangster era, the great Depression, World War II, Korea, and in between, forays into the development of the Iron Horse, the airplane, and the submarine. There were frequent side-trips (often quite critical) into British history, too. Reasonably accurate historically (in some cases remarkably so), these reconstructions of America's past have been more than a little colored by Ford's own viewpoints and attitudes. As a Naval officer, he has tended to make his service pictures strong on tradition and glory and condescending in their semi-comic treatment of the enlisted men. With the Western, however, he has taken the detached and rose-hued view typical of the non-Westerner. Although often authentic in detail, his Westerns as a whole were the exact opposite of William S. Hart's austere, hard-bitten, dusty ones. Both were poets in their fashion, but Hart offered a stark kind of poetry, whereas Ford's was warm and romanticized. Hart stressed the relationship between man and horse; Ford took the more epic and grander view by stressing man and the land. His films are full of panoramic long shots in which one is constantly reminded of man in relationship to his geographic environment, something that Hart (more concerned in his stories with individuals than with national expansion) never bothered himself with.

Ford's career began in 1914 as an actor and stuntman for his then more famous actor-director brother, Francis.

(Francis' career dwindled rapidly after the early 1920's, and he is today best remembered for the series of "lovable drunk" characterizations that he contributed to so many of John's films.) In 1917, however, Universal signed him to a director's contract, initially on two-reel Westerns, in one or two of which he starred himself. Still calling himself Jack, he was self-admittedly no actor, but Ford the director more than covered up for Ford the thespian, and in any event the films were constructed to place much greater emphasis on action and stunts than histrionics. His initial stars were Hoot Gibson and Harry Carey; within a few years, when he moved to Fox, he would be directing Tom Mix and Buck Jones. Because he served his apprenticeship on bread-and-butter actioners, Ford never forgot what audiences really wanted from Westerns—a lack of pretention and a maximum of action. Most of his later epic Westerns steadfastly refused to be overawed by their size, and continued to deliver the ingredients expected by the hard-core action fans. Even when occasionally shot down by a talkative and actionless script (1961's *Two Rode Together*), he kept his film visually on the move, playing out the long dialogue scenes on horseback or against picturesque locations.

Of Ford's twenty-eight films made for Universal between 1917 and 1921, only one is known to have survived. But European film archives are re-discovering "lost" American films all the time, frequently obscured through changed titles and lack of credits, so it is not altogether beyond hope that more of the early Fords may emerge in time. Obviously this was a tremendously important group of Westerns, since not only was Ford drawing the blueprints for his own later and more important works, but he was setting new standards in a style quite opposed to that of Hart, who was the only other film-maker devoting himself almost exclusively to the Western genre. Ford's plots were often quite strong and unusual, but always uncomplicated; action and photographic superiority were their common denominators. Critics who usually bypassed all of the non-William S. Hart Westerns made a point of singling out each new Ford, commenting on the steady improvement of Harry Carey as an actor under Ford's direction and Ford's own stress on magnificent locations and grade-A camerawork. In reviewing *The Outcasts of Poker Flat* (1919), *Photoplay* remarked, ". . . absolutely incomparable photography . . . this film is an optic symphony." (Subsequent versions of this Bret Harte tale were strong on talk and dramatics, decidedly weak on visuals.)

Very fortuitously, the *one* film from Ford's prolific early career that does still exist is his very first feature, *Straight Shooting,* made for Universal in 1917 and star-

Gloria Hope and
Cullen Landis in
The Outcasts of Poker Flat
(Universal, 1919)

ring Harry Carey and Hoot Gibson. Ford's own recollections of it are vague; clearly he has greater affection for *Marked Men* (1919), an early version of *Three Godfathers,* which he later remade with John Wayne. It's one of the few films before *The Iron Horse* that Ford will even talk about. Yet good as it undoubtedly must have been, it can hardly have been quite the milestone that *Straight Shooting* was. Not only was it his first full-length feature (a five-reeler), but since it was made in 1917, it is still very close to the beginning of his career. And for a film made by a man with literally only six months' directorial experience behind him, it is in many ways a remarkable film. Curiously, though, it is not at all what one would expect of an early Ford. His later penchant for slam-bang roistering action and low comedy, plus the fact that he had been working in two-reelers where the action was fast and the heroes rowdy (one of them even frequented a bordello for plot purposes!), would lead one to anticipate a rough-and-tumble actioner for his first feature. Yet its *Shane*-like plot—range war between cattlemen and homesteaders and the intervention on behalf of the homesteaders of a professional gunman—has surprising depth of characterization, and a rather slow, methodical build-up, punctuated by one burst of violent action at the mid-way point,

and then culminating in a spectacular and traditional finale: the shoot-out in the main street, the besieged homesteaders, and a ride to the rescue. There is a certain amount of influence from William S. Hart, but this is inevitable, since Hart's were the only major Westerns then being made. Tom Mix's Selig Westerns had been generally unimportant, and he didn't join Fox until 1917. Indeed, Mix's first Fox feature and Ford's first feature were made almost simultaneously and copyrighted only a week apart, so obviously it was much too early for Ford to have been influenced by Mix. The limited Hart influence can be seen in the general austerity of the production and in the characters themselves—good and bad intermingled in both the good guys and the bad guys, while Carey's characterization undoubtedly overlaps into Hart's "good badman" role. The sheriff (the only player too slick and Hollywood in his attire) is a nebulous and ineffectual character, and it is a gang of "good" outlaws (one of them "human" enough to steal a pot of jam from the heroine's larder!) who provide the posse for the last-minute rescue. But if its plot and deliberate striving for realism of detail are echoes of Hart, then there is also a showmanship and a production polish far more typical of the later Ford. It builds its excitement deliberately and in a steadily

50

Just Pals (Fox, 1921)
with Buck Jones
and ZaSu Pitts

The Iron Horse (Fox, 1924)

Fort Apache (RKO Radio, 1948): Typical boisterous Ford comedy;
Jack Pennick, Victor McLaglen, Dick Foran, Ward Bond

Stagecoach
(United Artists, 1939):
Ford's first use of
Monument Valley as a
location

rising tempo, in a manner that Hart usually avoided,
and it is unusually smooth in terms of composition,
camera set-ups, locations and lighting. It looks far more
like a production of 1922 than of 1917. Economies are
most skilfully carried off; for example, all of the cabin
interiors are shot on an outdoor stage, with just a flat
or two, but ingenious lighting, stressing the darkness "inside" and the sunlight outside through the framing of
doors and windows, makes them work beautifully. The
Devil's Canyon hideout of the outlaws (a narrow trail
through a deep gorge) is quite a familiar Ford location
by now; he used it again in *The Iron Horse* among other
films, and for the beginning of the Indian attack in
Stagecoach. The whole climax of the film suggests that
Ford had been more than casually impressed by the
climax of D. W. Griffith's *The Birth of a Nation*. Since
Ford recently revealed that he had ridden as one of the
Klansmen in those climactic reels, he obviously had a
first-hand opportunity to watch Griffith at work and
then see the results of that work in the finished film.
Not only in its construction but also in its composition,
Ford's climax is plainly related to Griffith's: the round-

ing up of the posse, the ride to the rescue, individual shots inside the besieged cabin (a gun barrel being pushed through the weakening door)—all of this heightened by the heroine (Molly Malone) making the most of a slight resemblance to Mae Marsh and imitating her as much as possible. Ford was astute enough to recognize not only *how* Griffith achieved certain effects, but also *why*. Thus, in the sequence of the cattlemen assembling their forces, saluting their leader, and riding into ranks, he copies exactly Griffith's composition in the parallel sequence of the assembly of the Klansmen. An apparently huge open field is "framed" by trees and foliage; not only is the composition pleasing, but a few riders thus concentrated into center-screen are able to suggest a much greater assemblage. Incidentally, a measure of the expertise of the climactic action and

The Horse Soldiers (United Artists, 1959)
Ford with Hoot Gibson

roundup scenes is that many of these scenes were still being used as stock shots in "B" Westerns of the late thirties and early forties.

Though it is easier for us to appreciate the importance of *Straight Shooting* in retrospect, since we can recognize in it so many of the roots of later Westerns, its merits were appreciated at the time by discerning critics. The trade paper *Moving Picture World* commented:

> . . . a clean-cut, straightforward tale. Both the author and the director are to be congratulated upon having selected compelling scenes and situations for the production. The Western panorama is set forth in clear, attractive photography and the riding and fighting episodes are enacted with dash and enthusiasm. So successful is the offering that it deserves to rank with *The Virginian* and *Whispering Smith*.

Ford's biggest silent Western epic, and indeed still one of the biggest Westerns from any period, was *The Iron Horse*, made some seven years later. Marred by a "B" picture script, it was still an epic in the fullest sense of the word, its action sequences splendidly staged and edited, a huge organizational undertaking for a man still in his late twenties! James Cruze's *The Covered Wagon*, made a year earlier and directly responsible for launching that first cycle of large-scale Westerns, was a primitive film by comparison, in every way (except photographically) inferior to Ford's. Yet even *The Iron Horse* must yield pride of place to *Three Badmen* (1926), Ford's last and best silent Western. Originally intended as a co-starring vehicle for Fox's three big action stars, Tom Mix, Buck Jones, and George O'Brien, it actually emerged with O'Brien as the nominal hero, and character-actors Tom Santschi, Frank Campeau and J. Farrell MacDonald in the larger roles of the title. With a beautifully staged landrush as its highlight, *Three Bad Men* was a unique blending of the austere and the traditional with the romanticized and the streamlined. Its heavily sentimental plot was pure William S. Hart and so were the characters; yet it was slammed over with a production gloss and a sense of humor that Hart had never achieved (or wanted). Rarely seen these days and generally unavailable even for archival showings in the United States, *Three Bad Men* is a major Ford work that should be revived if only within the limits of film societies and universities. Despite its popularity, it was Ford's last Western for thirteen years. His success in other areas (Americana, high adventure, crime and gangsterism) plus the apparent decline of the Western's popularity when sound came in, removed him from the

The Man Who Shot Liberty Valance (Paramount, 1962):
Ford with James Stewart and John Wayne

genre for the balance of his contract at Fox. The studio's "B" Westerns in the thirties (a George O'Brien series) were too unimportant to warrant his attention, and apart from Raoul Walsh's *The Big Trail* in 1930, Fox almost totally abandoned the big-budget Western between the advent of talkies and *Jesse James* in 1939. Not until his classic *Stagecoach* (made independently for Walter Wanger, also in 1939) did Ford return to the Western. Despite the renewed acclaim that it won for him and its huge commercial success (singlehandedly, it touched off the big new Western cycle of the early forties), Ford seemed to show no inclination to make any follow-ups. Only after his second talkie Western— *My Darling Clementine* in 1946, best of all the Wyatt Earp sagas and certainly one of Ford's best and most disciplined films—did he embrace the horse opera wholeheartedly again. The group that followed, many of them in color, included two of the permanent classics of the Western genre—*She Wore a Yellow Ribbon* (1949) and *The Wagon Master* (1950)—while the others: *Fort Apache* (1948), *Three Godfathers* (1948), *Rio Grande* (1950) *The Searchers* (1956), *The Horse Soldiers* (1959), *Sergeant Rutledge* (1960), *Two Rode Together* (1961), *The Man Who Shot Liberty Valance* (1962), *How the West Was Won* (1962) and *Cheyenne*

The Man Who Shot Liberty Valance: Ford directing a fight scene

Autumn (1964) constitute a remarkable and often closely interrelated series of essays on the Civil War and its aftermath, the Cavalry and its traditions, and the Indian wars and racial problems arising therefrom. Many American directors (King Vidor and Orson Welles are names that come most readily to mind) have made individual films superior to Ford's best, but no director, not even Griffith, maintained such a *consistently* high standard over such a long period of time—more than fifty years of active film-making. Ford has always been taken for granted, never honored as he should have been. In some ways this was all to the good, since Ford was enabled to go on making films the way *he* felt they should be made instead of, consciously or otherwise, catering to the demands of critics and cultists. His work has always been both a credit to the industry and an inspiration to other film-makers. Quite certainly, in the specific realm of the Western, it is impossible to over-emphasize the contribution he has made to the genre as a whole, or the beauty, poetry, and excitement he has brought to his own Western movies.

THE PRE-1920'S - AND TOM MIX

In view of William S. Hart's tremendous popularity, it is to be expected that many of the Westerns made in the period of his peak popularity, from 1916 to 1920, would attempt to cash in on both his personal image and his austere brand of film-making. Yet there was a remarkable variety in the Westerns that were turned out in this period. For one thing, of course, apart from the very occasional D. W. Griffith, Herbert Brenon, or Theda Bara spectacular, this was still well before the period of the "super" movie—and it was even longer before the period of the double bill. The average movie program consisted of the feature (usually five to seven reels in length), a slapstick comedy short, a travel or "interest" film, and possibly a serial episode. The West-

ern thus had to be capable of holding its own in competition with other features and had not yet become a staple "filler" of lesser commercial importance. Many stars, such as William Desmond and Roy Stewart, certainly specialized in Westerns above all others, while romantic stars such as William Farnum often proved to be so popular in Westerns that they stayed with them almost exclusively.

The popular serials of Pearl White and others often overlapped into Western territory, although the mystery story dominated the serials in the early period, and it wasn't until the twenties that the Western really became a major part of the serial field. Helen Holmes' popular railroading thrillers—first her *Hazards of Helen* one-reelers and later her features—likewise were usually done in the framework and setting of the Western, even though most of the action revolved around locomotives.

Furthermore, the Western could call on the strong and well-loved novels of Rex Beach, Owen Wister, Peter B. Kyne, and, above all, Zane Grey—stories that were fresh and were being brought to the screen for the first time. Some of the best of the early features were good just *because* they were Westerns, based on stories that were actionful and told in visual terms, thus presenting less of a challenge to fledgling screenwriters who still tended to construct "scenarios" in terms of tableaux and lists of shots.

Rex Beach's *The Spoilers,* filmed for the first time in 1914 by the Selig Company (and remade four times since) was a quite remarkable film for that date. Running for close to ninety minutes, it managed to avoid confusion despite a multiplicity of characters, created a creditably realistic picture of a muddy, brawling, gold-mining boom town, and was the first Western to build deliberately to a grand-scale fistic battle for its climax. Without doubles (and admittedly without some of the spectacular if improbable thrills that stuntmen could

have added), William Farnum and Tom Santschi put on a rousing fight that looked real all the way, and was climaxed by Farnum's victory and, as the Cavalry arrived to arrest the defeated villain, the classic line: "I broke him—with my hands." Only in its titling, in fact, did the film reveal any hesitancy, for every line of dialogue also identified the speaker, and sometimes when two-way conversations were reported on a single title there were two or three such identifications per title. Thus, it was like reading a page from a play, and for a moment one was taken entirely out of the movie. However, this literary echo lasted briefly; learning from Griffith, directors soon discovered how to edit so that audiences knew exactly who was saying what, without being told.

Griffith himself, having spent so much time with Westerns in his Biograph days, now had little interest in them. He produced (but did not direct) *Martyrs of the Alamo,* a historical Western that was the first feature to deal with the Sam Houston-Santa Ana conflict in Texas and Mexico, and he personally directed *Scarlet Days,* a Richard Barthelmess vehicle that was one of the pot-boilers he made between grander-scale endeavors in

Dustin Farnum and
Red Wing in *The Squawman*
(Famous Players,
Cecil B. DeMille, 1913)

58

order to keep product flowing and salaries paid. (Let it be noted, a Griffith potboiler was usually better than another director's super-special!) But, more's the pity, he never devoted himself to an important, large-scale Western spectacle to match *The Birth of a Nation* or *Orphans of the Storm,* although his 1924 *America,* dealing with the Revolutionary War on the Eastern seaboard, did contain many elements of the Western, and some of the biggest and best organized Indian fighting scenes ever filmed. Cecil B. DeMille made Westerns in this pre-1920 period, however, as did Henry King. King's Westerns, made for the American Film Company and starring William Russell, were curious in their anticipation of his best later Westerns. Like *The Gunfighter,* they stressed mood, tension, realism and naturalistic qualities far more than action. However, unlike *The Gunfighter,* their plots were fairly standard and *needed* action. King's early work was thus commendably off-beat, but not very successful, although the popularity of star William Russell carried them through. King was to find his true niche in the Americana of *Tol'able David* in 1921, and thereafter his best Westerns were those which stressed characterization and a feeling for time and place rather than melodrama and action.

Because appearing in a Western was a sure-fire way to build popularity and was far from the "slumming" it came to be regarded as later, many of the biggest stars of the pre-1920 era were ready and willing to appear in horse operas. Dustin Farnum had set the pattern with DeMille's *The Squawman,* and in his wake came J. Warren Kerrigan, Charles Ray, Harold Lockwood, and Wallace Reid. Mae Marsh made *The Wild Girl of the Sierras,* and another Griffith heroine—lovely and lively Dorothy Gish—kidded the genre beautifully in *Nugget Nell.*

Next to Charlie Chaplin (who never got closer to a Western, straight or otherwise, than *The Gold Rush)* the biggest stars of those years were Mary Pickford and Douglas Fairbanks, both of whom numbered Westerns among their biggest successes. (In fact, Mary's last film, the 1933 *Secrets,* was basically a Western, albeit an emotional one.) Pickford is too often shrugged aside as merely a sentimental, golden-curled figure. But while sentiment and pathos certainly figured in many of her films, so did stark drama, action, and even horror. There was nothing wishy-washy about our Mary, especially

J. Warren Kerrigan (center), a colorless star of actionless two-reel Westerns. In this unidentified circa 1914 film, Harold Lloyd (extreme right) is playing a bit.

Typical examples of independent 1914 Westerns prior to William S. Hart's establishment of a dynamic hero

Cameo of Yellowstone

prior to 1920, and her Westerns had a tremendous amount of vigor and sheer guts. *The Romance of the Redwoods* (directed by Cecil B. DeMille) had good Indian fighting scenes and plenty of strong drama, while in *M'liss* Mary rushes to rescue an innocent victim from a lynch mob, points out the actual miscreant, and looks on approvingly as he is taken off to be strung up from the nearest tree!

The Douglas Fairbanks Westerns were unique, and are still as fresh and delightful as they ever were. First at Triangle, and then later at Paramount, Doug was working on the same lot as William S. Hart. Hart took his Westerns very seriously, but occasionally when he wanted to let his hair down—only a trifle of course—he would do a story about the strong, silent Westerner who comes East with his strength and integrity to confound the city crooks. (*Branding Broadway* had him chasing the villain on horseback through Central Park.) Doug, on the other hand, never took his films seriously, and found in the West a perfect outlet for a modern tongue-in-cheek D'Artagnan. Thus Doug's scripts (usually written by Anita Loos and John Emerson) often found him as the cowboy-crazy Easterner, chained to a dull desk

Jerry and the Gunman

60

A Child of the Desert

job, wishing he had been born in an earlier age, and then going out West where he proves to be a tougher, rougher buckaroo than any of them. Such films as *Wild and Woolly, Manhattan Madness* and *Knickerbocker Buckaroo* enabled Doug to indulge in acrobatics, kid modern foibles, expound his optimistic philosophy (practical only if one had the unlimited funds to follow one's dreams instead of earning a living), and satirize Western clichés and traditions, all in one fell swoop. Doug's films moved like lightning, were as funny as they were thrilling, and had a grace, charm and zip that his later swashbucklers lacked. Mack Sennett had been satirizing Westerns for years, of course. Sennett's *His Bitter Pill,* with bulky Mack Swain lampooning Bill Hart, was a classic of its kind. Even Griffith, in his rural romance *Hoodoo Ann* (1916), has Mae Marsh and Bobby Harron go to a small-town movie house, where they see a Western with Carl Stockdale's hero a neat burlesque of Hart. The movie-within-a-movie also kidded what had already become clichés of carelessness and lack of continuity, such as the hero falling under a bullet so badly aimed that it couldn't have passed within six feet of him.

This kind of satire grew in number and subtlety as the Westerns themselves grew in popularity, reaching its height in the early twenties with Sennett's feature *Small Town Idol* (with Ben Turpin as a Western star returning to his Western home town) and Hal Roach's *Uncensored Movies,* in which Will Rogers does devastatingly accurate takeoffs on Bill Hart and Tom Mix. Fairbanks' satires, however, were on the Western genre as a whole, taking in the dime novel and the paintings of Frederick Remington for good measure, and they were wholeheartedly affectionate. Fairbanks loved the West as much as Hart, but he loved it for what it stood for rather than for what it was; he never romanticized it and was shrewd enough to include a scene near the end of his films where he admitted he had been a fool, whereupon the level-headed Westerners (and the heroine) accepted him for what he was.

Even the great Fatty Arbuckle made a Western during this period, and oddly enough it wasn't a knockabout spoof. *The Roundup* had a relatively straightforward story (the same studio, Paramount, remade it early in the forties) and Arbuckle was praised for his acting. Actually in a secondary role, he played a genial sheriff

61

much in the manner of Eugene Pallette in the talkies.

As the teen-years rolled on towards the twenties, the star system began to assert and categorize itself, and it became apparent that certain stars would always enjoy their greatest popularity in Westerns. Universal had developed Hoot Gibson and Harry Carey. Roy Stewart, Triangle's follow-up star to William S. Hart, had none of Hart's creativity or individual style, but still built quite a following. Franklyn Farnum, in two-reelers, seemed to be another star to watch, but his career never really took off, and it was a supporting player in those shorts—Buck Jones—who achieved real fame.

Fans were irked by stars who, on their own or at their studio's insistence, gave themselves names which suggested kinship with established stars: Neal Hart, William Fairbanks. Even though some of these stars were attractive personalities, and as actors and action performers often superior to others, the ingrained resentment against them remained and their careers were usually brief and limited to quickie productions. Nevertheless, their presence served to help establish the beginning of the roster of players who would devote themselves exclusively to Westerns, a roster, and a genre, that was given tremendous impetus by the advent of the most popular Western star of them all, Tom Mix.

When Mix ultimately became a big star at Fox, pub-

The Universal studios then, as now, made an extra dollar by letting in tourists! Here they watch the shooting of a Harry Carey Western of 1917 vintage

Wild and Woolly (Paramount, 1917) with Douglas Fairbanks

Deuce Duncan (Triangle, 1917)
with William Desmond and Luella Maxim

Keith of the Border (Triangle, 1917)
with Roy Stewart

Last of the Duanes (Fox, 1918) with William Farnum

M'liss (Paramount, 1918) with Mary Pickford and Thomas Meighan

licity created a biography for him far more colorful than any of his movie roles. But no matter how exaggerated this may have been, there is no doubt that he did have a rugged and adventurous life prior to his movie days, seeing action with the Army in the Spanish-American War and the Philippine insurrection, breaking horses for the British for use against the Boers in Africa, and serving for a period as a deputy United States marshal in Oklahoma. He had also been a champion rodeo rider and performer with the Miller Brothers 101 Ranch Show. So with all this material to draw upon, it is not surprising that Fox's publicity department built him up into a composite of Wyatt Earp and D'Artagnan!

Actually, with so much activity (and three of his five wives) behind him, Mix was on the point of settling down to sedate ranch life when he entered into a minor business deal with the Selig Company. They were about to shoot a semi-documentary short entitled *Ranch Life in the Great South West,* and Mix offered his ranch, livestock, and advisory services. The project was finished and apparently forgotten; Mix had no great interest in

pursuing a career in movies. Later, however, the Selig people contacted him again, offered him a rather vague job in which he would handle livestock, double for actors in tricky action scenes, and generally advise in the production of a series of Westerns. Mix accepted, and was permanently assigned to the company's California studio. Although active and, for a while prosperous, Selig was a minor company in terms of creativity or concrete contributions to the development of film. They specialized in Westerns, jungle pictures, and contemporary crime stories. Unlike the Biograph, Ince, and Vitagraph studios, they nurtured but few embryonic talents. Mix was the only really big name ever to emerge from an apprenticeship there. However, between 1911 and 1917—the period of William S. Hart's ascendancy, and of Broncho Billy Anderson's rise and decline—Mix made almost a hundred films, primarily one- and two-reelers, for Selig. Initially they were artless, off-the-cuff affairs, loosely strung together without scripts, and concentrating as much on folksy comedy in the Will Rogers vein as on traditional action. (Mix had been a friend of

Rogers, and may well have deliberately tried to cultivate a Rogers "image" for himself since Rogers had, as yet, shown no inclination to try the movies himself.) On many of the films, Mix was star, author and director, an ambitious undertaking for one with such a modicum of creative and business ability in his background. If for nothing else, Mix deserves credit for turning out so much product so regularly. Too, his films improved as they went along. Mix gradually dropped the stress on comedy *(Why the Sheriff Is a Bachelor)* in favor of vehicles which really allowed him to display his riding and stunting prowess *(The Stagecoach Driver and the Lady, Pony Express Rider).*

Many of the early entries in the series were simple comedies or dramas about the making of Westerns—a cunning way of making movies with even less set dressing than usual—and some of them, like *Sagebrush Tom* (the cowboys decide to stage a Western version of *Quo Vadis?)* have added historic value today in that they have thus preserved detailed coverage of the Selig working methods, shots of camera equipment, even closeups of studio note-paper with instructions to the crew. But as a group, the Tom Mix Westerns were generally mild and inferior to such Selig "specials" as *The Spoilers* or a 1913 William Duncan vehicle, *The Range Law.* Mix did graduate into features under Selig, but most of them were loosely assembled and padded with too much bantering comedy. Later, with Mix a big name star at Fox, Selig created "new" Mix features like *Twisted Trails* by taking old shorts and, with considerable ingenuity, re-editing and re-titling them into five-reel features. After devoting considerable footage to heroine Bessie Eyton from a non-Mix film, they finally meet (in a scene from one of their two-reelers) and a title informs us "Thus were the twisted trails of the boy and girl joined together!" With the exception of 1914's *Chip of the Flying U,* which had a good original story (by Peter B. Kyne) and a good director (Colin Campbell, who also directed *The Spoilers* that same year) none of Mix's Selig films made much impression. On the other hand, relatively few of them are extant for reappraisal today, so it is unfair to condemn them all out of hand. But since they failed to make Mix a big star over a six-year period, one can safely assume that the majority of them were routine at best.

However, Mix's rugged riding and action skills had attracted the attention of Fox executives. Fox, then perhaps the biggest of all the studios, offered Mix a contract and, he went to work for them in 1917. Although his first trial balloon there was a two-reeler that he wrote and directed himself *(Six Cylinder Love),* he immediately thereafter switched to full features, and left

Tom Mix

65

The Cyclone (Fox, 1920)
with Tom Mix, Colleen Moore

the direction to veterans better qualified to handle it: Chester and Sidney Franklin, Lynn Reynolds, Lambert Hiller. From the beginning, Mix was handled as a unique property, designed to be as different from the reigning Western king, William S. Hart, as possible. His films were to include liberal doses of comedy and small-child appeal. (Youngsters undoubtedly adored Hart for a while, but he made no attempt to cultivate their continued favor by including elements in his films expressly designed to please them.) Furthermore, they were to be rugged and action-packed, but essentially non-violent. Gradually a deliberate kind of "circus" format was created for the Mix films. They were full of fights and chases, essentially realistic in such details as costuming and locations, but emphatically escapist in dramatic terms. No serious issues were ever raised by the Mix plots, and nobody was expected to take them too seriously. As their popularity increased, so did their story-lines tend to become even less realistic. Tom's plots provided him with sojourns in Arabia and Ruritania. Essentially up-to-the-minute, they concentrated on modern speed—locomotives, racing cars, ocean liners, airplanes were frequently incorporated into his stories as props on which even more action could be hung. Only twice did Mix really misfire, once in *Dick Turpin* (fans would not accept him out of Western costume or, even sympathetically, on the wrong side of the law as the British highwayman), and again in *Riders of the Purple Sage.* This mid-twenties adaptation of the Zane Grey novel was a perfect example of the wrong kind of vehicle for Mix. A strong, dramatic yarn that would have been ideally suited for Hart, it presented Mix as a revenge-obsessed wanderer. Its complicated story-line left too little room for action, and the three-dimensional Mix character *had* to be taken seriously and believed in.

But the bulk of his pictures avoided these mistakes. Action rather than logic remained the keynote, and Mix went out of his way to devise elaborate stunt sequences (most of which he performed without doubles) or bits of business which could spotlight action but never gratuitous violence. Despite horrendous threats by the villains, the death-rate in the Mix films was practically nil. He would subdue a victim with his fists or with some fancy lasso work, rarely by shooting him, and never by killing him. In contrast, William S. Hart was a deadly, no-nonsense avenger behind a pair of six-guns, and even Douglas Fairbanks, in his spoof *Wild and Woolly,* casually shot the unarmed captured villain in the knee to make him "stay put" while he rode off to rescue the heroine! Mix's unlikely but likeable hero, clean-living to a fault, possessed of no vices (certainly not smoking and drinking) and all the virtues, was not

66

absurd in his own make-believe world, and for a long time to come set the pattern of behavior for all Western heroes. Since he always delivered the entertainment goods in terms of good stories and lively action, no one quibbled at his radical departure from the previous traditions laid down by Hart. Moreover, Mix's films were always good to look at. He used the best cameramen available (Dan Clark was his most frequently used) and made a point of shooting many of his films amid the stunning scenery of the national parks. *Sky High,* for example, was shot almost entirely in and around the Grand Canyon, its action ranging from a rugged fight on the banks of the churning Colorado River to exciting and precarious chases along the narrow trails lining the chasm walls and aerial stunting in a plane skimming the rim of the canyon. Together with *Just Tony, The Great K and A Train Robbery* (using the Denver and Rio Grande Railroad, this contained some of Mix's best and most elaborate stunts), *The Lone Star Ranger* and *The Rainbow Trail, Sky High* was one of Mix's best.

By the mid-twenties, Mix was earning a salary of seventeen thousand dollars a week—and living it up accordingly! However, he more than earned it. Fox, no longer as successful as it had been in the pre-1920 era, needed the huge profits from the Mix pictures. Without them, such classic films as *Sunrise*—the kind of film that every studio wanted to make for "prestige" purposes, even though they could never show a real profit—could not have been made.

Despite their huge success, Fox and Mix (the guiding impresario behind his own films, though he only physically directed two of his more than sixty films for the studio) were wise enough not to tamper with their formula. Even at his peak, Mix limited himself to five- and six-reel features that really *moved* and gave the fans just what they wanted. No pretention ever crept into his films, though with their success assured, more money was occasionally allocated to get top directors (John Ford made two of the Mix features) and strong supporting casts. But not a nickel was ever spent on weigh-

Hello Cheyenne
(Fox, 1928)
with Mix

Uncensored Movies (Pathé, 1923): Will Rogers satirizing Mix

ing down the star with "art" in the form of décor or complicated plot structure.

This was a lesson that Republic Studios, number-one makers of Westerns in the talkie era, several times failed to remember. Having built Bill Elliott into a top Western star via a series of expert and fast-moving "B"s, they changed Bill to William and promoted him to nine-reel historical western "special," in which he was tied down by frock coats and silk shirts, reels of dialogue, studio "exteriors" and back projection, and far too little fresh air, horses, and wagons. Expensive films like *In Old Sacramento* and *The Plainsman and the Lady* contained not a quarter of the action or appeal of his five-reelers, and he lost much of his popularity until he reverted to his former style—and scale—with a good "B" series for Monogram. To a degree, Republic made the same mistake with Roy Rogers and Gene Autry, too, though they remedied it before too much damage was done.

But Fox learned its lesson very quickly with *Dick Turpin* and *Riders of the Purple Sage,* and never let Mix step out of his class. The result was the most consistently satisfying and commercially successful series of "small" Westerns in the history of the movies. They sounded the death-knell for William S. Hart, rapidly overtaking him in popularity. He neither could nor wanted to compete, and gradually, though with distinction and honor, he let himself be eased out of the movies, to be replaced not only by Mix himself, but by the new breed of cowboy he had brought to the screen. Two of the best of them, Buck Jones and George O'Brien, came from the ranks of Mix's own crews, while by the early twenties, many others—Hoot Gibson, Fred Thomson, Ken Maynard, Tim McCoy, Yakima Canutt—were ready to cash in on and expand the streamlined new format that Mix had established. The austerity of Hart and his "strong, silent" image were too firmly entrenched to be entirely dismissed, and his breed of Westerner still had its loyal following. Hart himself remained in Westerns until 1925, and Harry Carey, Jack Holt, Art Acord and a handful of others continued to make Westerns in the Hart manner. But, for the most part, Mix had succeeded in establishing a formula both for the series-Western and for the Western hero that would remain unchanged until the small Western itself bit the dust in the mid-1950's, scalped by the impossible odds of rising production costs and driven off their ranges by the inroads of television, just as surely as the Red Indians had been decimated by the coming of the Iron Horse and the slaughter of the buffalo herds.

Ruth Mix, Tom's daughter, who starred in several Westerns in the late twenties and early thirties.

THE FIRST EPICS

Although the huge popularity of the Tom Mix Westerns certainly increased the box-office value of the horse opera and stimulated more production in the area of the two-reeler, it did not materially increase the number of feature-length Westerns being made. That catharsis came in 1923 with Paramount's production of *The Covered Wagon*. Based on a novel by Emerson Hough, it initially was put into production as a result of the success of William S. Hart's *Wagon Tracks*. Made very largely on location, with relatively minor stars (its biggest name, Mary Miles Minter, had withdrawn to be replaced by Lois Wilson), it almost unwittingly grew into epic proportions, and in fact became the first real super-Western. Its success with both critics and public

was instantaneous, although it does not survive the years well, and today seems a disappointing and unexciting film. Yet it *is* one of the key Western films, one of perhaps no more than half-dozen that have made a major contribution to the development of the genre. Some, like *Stagecoach,* made that contribution in an artistic or commercial sense. *The Covered Wagon,* on the other hand, is a "milestone" film, supremely important in that by being made at all it introduced the epic tradition to the Western, and gave it scale and poetic and documentary values. Thanks mainly to the grandeur and panoramic beauty of Karl Brown's camerawork, it is easy to understand why it so captured the imagination of audiences in 1923. John Ford's *The Iron Horse* of

1924 is as entertainment far more exciting and as film far more creative, but it undoubtedly owes its existence to the prior success of *The Covered Wagon*.

The major liability of *The Covered Wagon* lies in the work of James Cruze, who was one of the most successful and highest-paid directors of the silent screen, and whose simple, uncomplicated style found a certain favor then. But in retrospect one can see that almost all of his silents were far superior in theme and content to execution, and almost without exception were stoogy, plodding, unimaginative works. This is especially true of his big epics of American history (including *Old Ironsides* and the talkie *Sutter's Gold*), although oddly enough, some of his less ambitious silents and later, relatively unimportant talkies, revealed real talent and filmic flair. Cruze used little of the basic grammar of the film, and *The Covered Wagon* seems an especially dull film in comparison with Griffith's *Orphans of the Storm* of the previous year. He seldom moved his camera, and even the usually foolproof runaway horse sequence is, in *The Covered Wagon,* handled in one single long shot (exactly, in fact, as Edwin S. Porter had handled a runaway horse sequence in *Life of an American Policeman* in 1905, except that even Porter had the instinct to break it up into a series of static long shots). Cruze

likewise cared nothing for the cumulative effect of editing, and the Cavalry's ride to the rescue is almost as staid and matter-of-fact as the lacklustre ride in Edison's *The Corporal's Daughter,* discussed earlier, though sheer size was something of a saving grace with Cruze. And despite automatically recreating the conditions of an old wagon train trek, Cruze also seemed indifferent to the demands of realism. If he couldn't shoot genuine riding closeups on location, then better none at all than the patently phony ones (a man bobbing up and down on a barrel against a moving cycloramic background) utilized in the buffalo hunt sequence. And as Bill Hart observed somewhat contemptuously, no wagonmaster worth his salt would camp his train in a box canyon in the heart of Indian territory! Even allowing for the fact that the film was started as a programmer and the script rewritten and enlarged in production as it became apparent that this would emerge as a "big" picture, it contains some very barren writing. There is no vital, dramatic sense of opening up new frontiers; even the period is a bit hazy, and the subtitles constantly fall back on dates and gratuitous references to Lincoln and Brigham Young as a means of documenting what is going on. Nor is the cinematic reconstruction of the period helped by the balance between incidents; a con-

Karl Brown shooting the main title for *The Covered Wagon* (Paramount, 1923)

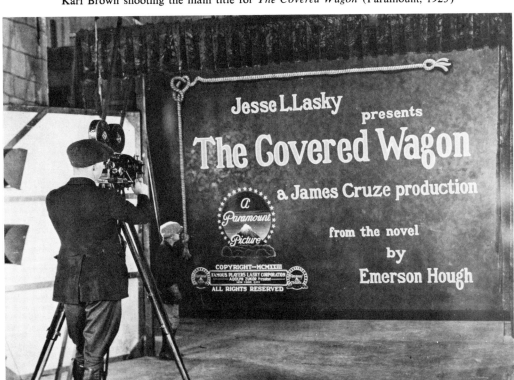

Director James Cruze
technical advisor
Tim McCoy, and one of the
Indian chiefs used in
The Covered Wagon

ventional fight between hero and villain is given far more prominence than the discovery of gold in California, which is treated in a completely offhand manner.

But much of the scope and richness of the film's visual tapestry does still have power, as does the superb work of Ernest Torrence and Tully Marshall as the two old scouts. The panoramic scenes of the wagon train, the near-documentary footage of campfire-singing, a burial, a river-crossing and the hazards of snow and mud, are still stirring and pictorially very beautiful. (A prairie fire sequence was cut after the initial road-show runs, probably because it was so brief and prosaic as to be merely frustrating in the framework of an epic.) But filmically stagnant though it may seem today, *The Covered Wagon* must still rank with *The Great Train Robbery,* the first works of William S. Hart, and Ford's *Stagecoach* as one of the most influential Westerns of all time. Its place in film history is an important one, even if its place in film art is limited to the camerawork of Karl Brown. And its place in the commercialization of the Western speaks for itself. The year prior to its release saw the production of a mere fifty Western features, and apart from the Mix and Hart films most of these were relatively unimportant programmers with such stars as Francis Ford and Roy Stewart, while even

the better non-star Westerns, such as King Vidor's underrated and charming *The Sky Pilot,* created little stir.

But in the year following the release of *The Covered Wagon,* the number of Westerns in circulation was tripled. The biggest and most successful of all the follow-ups was, of course, John Ford's *The Iron Horse,* made for Fox. It succeeded in developing the sense of urgency and pride in national progress that had been largely absent from Cruze's film, and it was to be of considerable influence on such later films as DeMille's *Union Pacific,* the British *The Great Barrier* (about the building of the Canadian Pacific Railroad), and the Russian *Turksib,* while the many lesser and standardized railroad Westerns of the fifties—*Kansas Pacific, Santa Fe, The Denver and the Rio Grande,* and others—inevitably, if not intentionally, derived much from it.

Although *The Iron Horse* was his first spectacular, Ford had already made almost forty Westerns. While this was an epic in every sense of the word, he wasn't overawed by the importance of his work. It is big and massive and yet, unlike so many historical super-Westerns (especially Frank Lloyd's *Wells Fargo*), it doesn't allow itself to slow down into stiff tableaux. The action, though a trifle slow in starting, is rugged and vigorous. The climax with its massed Indian fighting, the locomotive racing men to the rescue, and hero and villain settling matters with a personal fistic bout, is one of the most exciting such sequences ever put on film. If anything, its epic theme is occasionally marred by Ford's great affection for the smaller Western, his insistence on milking raucous slapstick scenes for more than they are worth, and a basic plot-line (a man's search through the years for his father's murderer) lifted from any grade-"B" Western.

Ford emulated Cruze and *The Covered Wagon* by shooting almost all of his film, under great hardships, on location. There is a minimum of studio work, and the film was completed under much the same conditions as the original Union Pacific railroad, the unit building itself complete towns as it moved along and using a train of fifty-six coaches for transportation. But otherwise, Ford's film was the very antithesis of Cruze's stiff one with its deliberate underplaying of the big action highlights. Cruze's big Indian battle had been sharp, massive, but almost casually thrown away, with no attempt to build excitement. He would get one shot of charging Indians and then forget them. Ford, on the other hand, shot his riders from all angles, intercut them, built his excitement steadily, and constantly changed the vantage point of his cameras. Despite its superior action content, *The Iron Horse* did not duplicate the great critical acclaim of *The Covered Wagon,* but it did enjoy huge popular success, ran for a year at the Lyric in New York, and won the praise and endorsement of governmental and educational bodies. One 1924 critic

Awaiting the Indian attack in a box canyon: *The Covered Wagon*

termed it "An American Odyssey," a phrase that seems peculiarly appropriate to so many of Ford's films of Americana.

Oddly enough, the dual success of these two initial epic Westerns did not spur a whole cycle of similar follow-ups, and the documenting of Wells Fargo and Western Union and of the taming of Dodge City, Wichita, and other frontier towns, all had to await the coming of the sound film. To be truly successful in a commercial sense, the epic needs to feed off a feeling of national pride and patriotism, and in return can perform propagandist as well as entertainment services. It is no coincidence that the most effective of the Western epics were made in periods when America most needed a sense of national pride and a rekindling of the pioneer spirit—during the early days of the Depression and at the beginning of World War II. It can be argued that America certainly needed that sense of national pride during the twenties, but the film can only reflect it, not create it. The twenties were an era of moral and legal upheaval, when it was deemed smart to take a drink merely because it was against the law, and when divorce and Freud were considered the sophisticated subjects for conversation. In such a milieu, and against a background of fun and plenty, appeals to national pride seemed Victorian and old-fashioned, and films which took a patriotic stand were automatically deemed quaint and out-of-date. (Ironically, most of them have survived rather well, and it is the "modern" sophisticated films of the twenties that tend to date most of all.) Griffith's *America* (dealing with the Revolutionary War) was a casualty of this atmosphere, and the consensus was that the Cruze and Ford epics had scored on their action, their size, perhaps even on their beauty and poetry, but not on their themes.

This seemed to be confirmed when James Cruze followed up *The Covered Wagon* with another historical Western, *The Pony Express*. Again, it was a stiff and disjointed film. There were too many characters, too much interweaving of a stereotyped fictional story with involved political history. The action—particularly a big Indian raid for the climax—was big and impressive, but

Shooting *The Covered Wagon* in Snake Valley, Nevada

Shooting *The Covered Wagon* in Snake Valley, Nevada

John Ford directs Iron Eyes Cody (right) in *The Iron Horse* (Fox, 1924)

The Iron Horse: George O'Brien, Madge Bellamy

The Iron Horse: George O'Brien, J. Farrell MacDonald

The Pony Express (Paramount, 1925), directed by Cruze, with Ernest Torrence, Ricardo Cortez, George Bancroft

The Thundering Herd (Paramount, 1925), directed by William K. Howard, with Raymond Hatton, Jack Holt, Lois Wilson

Tumbleweeds (United Artists, (1925); the opening of the Cherokee Strip

again unexciting. The most interesting aspect of the film was the surprisingly accurate use of Jack Slade (played by George Bancroft) as the villain. Not only did he manage to turn most situations to his advantage and emerge triumphant, prosperous, and unpunished at the end, but he even contrived to have a hapless Indian henchman hauled off and lynched by the populace to cover up his crimes! (An interesting and unorthodox character, Slade was later the subject of a reasonably honest if somewhat neurotic biography in the fifties, with Mark Stevens both playing the role and directing the film.) However, the failure of *The Pony Express* can't altogether be laid to its limitations as a film. Although bogged down in plot complications and lacking the sustained visual sweep of *The Covered Wagon,* it wasn't spectacularly inferior to it. The public obviously was not sympathetic to the epic as a genre. But *The Covered Wagon* had established a market for the big-scale Western, and Hollywood exploited it to the full. Although

Three Badmen (Fox, 1926), directed by John Ford; with Tom Santschi, J. Farrell MacDonald, Frank Campeau

Flaming Frontier (Universal, 1926): Harold Goodwin, Anne Cornwall, player, George Fawcett, Hoot Gibson

Paramount filmed other Emerson Hough novels—most successfully, *North of '36,* a direct sequel to *The Covered Wagon,* but with the stress on a virile action star in Jack Holt and a director (Irvin Willat) who was a specialist in thrills and movement—they switched their emphasis to a long-running series of Zane Grey adaptations. Where these had built-in epic qualities, as in *The Vanishing American,* a Richard Dix "special," they were deliberately minimized and reshaped to formula Western level. Universal's *Flaming Frontier,* dealing with Custer's Last Stand, was sold not on its epic qualities, but on its star cast (Dustin Farnum, Hoot Gibson, and others) and on its spectacular action. 1925 set a new high-water mark in the number of Westerns, big and small, that

Hollywood had produced. New stars were emerging to meet the demand; prominent directors-to-be (William K. Howard, William Wyler, W. S. Van Dyke) were learning their trade in the best school of all—making Western films that *moved,* making them fast, and making them cheaply; and the quickie producers were coming in, like sooners in a landrush, capitalizing on a great and suddenly popular genre, cheapening it, hastening the arrival of the double-bill program. The genuine epic was temporarily pushed aside, but the Western as a popular form of mass entertainment was launched and established as never before, with a whole host of new Western stars joining Tom Mix in the stampede to the nation's box offices.

The Winning of Barbara Worth (Goldwyn-United Artists, 1926), directed by Henry King; Vilma Banky, Ed Brady, Gary Cooper

Jesse James (Paramount, 1927), with Fred Thomson

STARS OF THE TWENTIES

Almost anything can be "proved" by statistics. In the sixties, the television rating specialists could show that on a given night *x*-million viewers saw a specific television Western, and since that exceeded the number that saw any given theatrical Western with Tom Mix, then, Q.E.D., that television star is automatically the most popular Western star of all time! Forgotten are such intangibles as the fact that the show might have been the best of several mediocrities available that night, that ninety per cent of those who tuned in might have tuned out again five minutes later, that they didn't have to pay or exert themselves in any way, and that once the ratings fell and the series was cancelled, that fantastically popular Western star might never be heard of again!

The relative failure of such popular TV cowboys as Hugh O'Brian and James Arness in theatrical Westerns is proof positive that genuine popularity has to be earned. Stars of the twenties really had to work for and earn first their stardom, and then their popularity—but that popularity, once earned, was never lost. Moviegoers of the silent days offered genuine love and admiration to their favorites, not merely manufactured overnight idolatry. They picked the star whose work or whose type of Western most appealed to them, and they remained loyal through the bad pictures as well as the good. Children who grew up on Ken Maynard or Hoot Gibson in the twenties may have seen fewer Westerns as they grew to maturity, but they would always remember them with genuine affection and spring to their defense when the latest singing cowboy was hailed as the successor to their throne.

The redoubtable Ida Belaney of Brooklyn is an example: a lady with an amazing recall of *all* the Buck Jones films, including the ones where he doubled or stunted for Tom Mix, the plot-lines, the dialogue in the talkies. How many television watchers, four decades hence, can be expected to demonstrate such erudite devotion to the careers of Clint Eastwood or Wayne Maunder? The innate good judgment of the moviegoing public has always been underrated. That public discovered Fairbanks, Chaplin, Pickford, and Laurel & Hardy long before the critics did, and that same public made deserved stars of Tom Mix, Fred Thomson and Buck Jones, rejecting those who had nothing to offer—Al Hoxie, Don Coleman, Dick Hatton, Fred Humes. While the mediocrities deservedly fell by the wayside, the line-up of Western stars in the twenties was so rich and varied that many who were deserving of success, but lacked that little extra individual something, likewise failed to make the grade. Wally Wales (who later renamed himself Hal Taliaferro) and Edmund Cobb were two athletic, able, and likeable stars whose pictures were usually enjoyable, but who never made even the second echelon of stars. They became better known as character actors and villains in the sound era, Wales in particular developing a distinctive make-up, costuming and speaking style that made him instantly recognizable. Small wonder that stars like these and Bob Custer, Jack Perrin, Guinn Williams and Tex (later Kermit) Maynard made little headway in the face of such an onslaught of Western stars from the early twenties on.

Fred Thomson was the closest rival to Mix. His initial Western series, made for FBO, was carefully patterned after the Mix formula: lighthearted, fast, filled with stunt action (Thomson was a splendid athlete, and used few doubles), and backed by top directors and cameramen. They were handsome to look at and they moved like lightning. Thomson was a rugged, goodlooking fellow who had studied for the priesthood, and because of this he stressed strong moral values, avoided sex and undue violence, intended his films to be a good influence on youth as well as entertaining them, and often worked in subplots (one involving the Boy Scouts, for example) that he felt would be meaningful to youngsters. At times he went even farther than Mix with his action sequences, emulating Fairbanks in bringing in (as in *Thundering Hoofs*) comedy or action stunt sequences that were quite extraneous to the basic plot-line. And while Mix usually dressed fairly realistically on screen, reserving his expensive uniform-costumes for personal appear-

Buck Jones

Hoot Gibson

Fred Thomson

Jack Hoxie

Tim McCoy

Ken Maynard

William Desmond

ances, Thomson constantly wore colorful costumes that smacked more of the rodeo than the range. His career was tragically brief; after the expiration of his FBO contract, he moved to Paramount to star in Western specials, of which *Jesse James* is the best remembered, but died suddenly at the peak of his popularity.

Art Acord is a prime example of the star whose reputation has been sustained almost solely by his legions of loyal devotees. Almost nothing is left of Acord's work today; we can see him playing two different extra roles in the early Ince film *The Indian Massacre,* and we can see one or two of his last, cheap, independent films like *Fighters of the Saddle.* A man of short stature, with a weatherbeaten face in the Harry Carey tradition, he shows little real star quality in these films from the extreme ends of his career. Yet, in his big Universal serials and Western specials in the intervening years, he proved to be another major rival to Mix.

Jack Hoxie was a player of restricted talent and variable pictures, and his huge popularity must be attributed to the fact that he made more good pictures than bad ones and that when they were good, they were *very* good. He had started out as Hart Hoxie, made an interesting but not very actionful series of "B" Westerns (off-beat to say the least, one of them even having a dream sequence with pixies!) and then joined Universal in 1924. Hoxie was a big, amiable oaf, whose large frame made him seem clumsy afoot and whose expression suggested that his mind was a complete blank except when the director told him to pantomime a specific emotion. But on a horse, he was something else again, an expert rider and stunter. His first film for Universal, *Don Quickshot of the Rio Grande,* fortunately kept him on his horse most of the time, and provided him with some elaborate stunts, leaps, transfers from galloping horse to moving train. A tongue-in-cheek frolic, it took nothing seriously, but it *moved* from the first scene to the last, and was beautifully photographed against majestic exteriors. Its opening was an elaborate dream sequence lampooning the days of King Arthur's knights. (If nothing else, the film seems to have impressed Ken Maynard a great deal, since he obviously based his *The Grey Vulture* of 1925 on it, even to copying the dream-knighthood opening.) But Hoxie needed constant speed, anything to prevent his getting off his horse and acting. When he was given a serious Western, as in *Back Trail* (directed by Bill Hart's old crony, Cliff Smith, and with a slow-moving, sentimental story of regeneration that would have been better suited to Hart), he fell down badly. Since he was one of the biggest Western moneymakers in the twenties, obviously he made few Westerns like *Back Trail.* Hoxie could neither read nor write, and

genially accepted some rather cruel inside jokes about those failings in several of his films. The inability to read, remember, or deliver a line defeated him when sound came in, and, unable to handle even the tatty dialogue of the grade-Z quickies like *Valley of Gold,* he drifted out of the movies.

Hoot Gibson, after starring in John Ford features, found himself "promoted" downstairs into a series of highly popular two-reelers for Universal in the early twenties. Western two-reelers were plentiful then and full of action; Gibson's decision was to develop a slow, bantering comedy style, with little action (to emphasize this, he never wore a gun-belt, and if he ever had to use a gun, usually borrowed one and stuck it in his boot) and simple story-lines. Because of their sheer novelty, and Gibson's ingratiating style—plus the fact that he *was* an ex-rodeo champ and could deliver the action goods when required—these shorts were extremely popular. Gibson was soon returned to features, but retained his emphasis on comedy. His early features were

Bob Steele

83

Wally Wales (later Hal Taliaferro)

Leo Maloney

Edmund Cobb

Buffalo Bill, Jr. (J. C. Wilsey)

Fred Humes

Buddy Roosevelt   Ted Wells

The Fighting Shepherdess (Vitagraph, 1920), with Anita Stewart, Wallace MacDonald

85

extremely good, slow-moving openings amply compensated for by dynamic endings, as in *The Phantom Bullet,* with its last-reel fight, chase, and a spectacular stunt of an auto diving from a high cliff into a lake. However, the Gibson series deteriorated towards the end of the twenties. Action content got even less, the comedy was padded by bantering dialogue titles; and the slim plots grew slimmer. *King of the Rodeo* was a bland bore except for an enjoyable last-reel sequence of Gibson chasing through the streets of Chicago on a motorcycle.

One of the most likeable Western stars of the twenties was Ken Maynard, who came to the screen via a bit in a Fox Buck Jones Western, attracted notice as Paul Revere in *Janice Meredith,* made some cheap independent films which were fast on action and long on displays of Maynard's riding skill, and finally landed a contract for a series of eighteen Westerns at First National. They placed action and streamlined production values before all else, and in terms of excitement and sheer size were some of the best program Westerns ever made. Their plots may have been skimpy, but they had the mountings of a *Stagecoach*—extensive location shooting, big action scenes, no stinting in extras, horses or wagon-power. When the script called for a mad stampede of fifty covered wagons, they got them, and not

just a half-dozen carefully intercut with old stock shots. Al Rogell, who also worked on the Fred Thomsons at FBO, directed the best of them, and their superior camerawork utilized several camera trucks to their fullest advantage, providing continuous speed and variety of angle in all of the running inserts. Moreover, Maynard himself was at his physical peak: slim, handsome, and an incredible trick and stunt rider. Most of his riding stunts, leaps and falls were shot in closeup, precluding the possibility of doubles. Maynard was a clumsy actor with dialogue, often given to rather bizarre ad-libs, and seldom able to achieve the subtlety of underplaying a key dramatic or comic line. But for those few silent years at First National he was in his prime, and everying a good Western star should be. The care that went into films like *Red Raiders* more than paid off in an unexpected way: for years First National were able to build their talkie "B" Westerns (first a series with John Wayne and subsequently one with Dick Foran) around the spectacular action from these Maynards, and when they abandoned "B" Westerns in the late thirties, they continued to sell this footage to Columbia and other companies.

Some measure of the remarkable quality of these films can be gathered from the fact that *Red Raiders,*

The Fighting Shepherdess (Vitagraph, 1920) with Anita Stewart, Wallace MacDonald

King Vidor directing John Bowers and Colleen Moore at Truckee locations for *The Sky Pilot* (First National, 1921)

Shooting a runaway buggy sequence for an independent Western, 1924

Bela Lugosi as the heroic
Uncas in a German version
of *Last of the Mohicans*
(1922)

William Farnum in
Brass Commandments
(Fox, 1923)

Art Acord and the horse "Raven" in *The Circus Cyclone*
(Universal, 1925)

Buck Jones and Marion Nixon in *Durand of the Badlands*
(Fox, 1925)

Bob Custer in *A Man of Nerve* (FBO, 1925)

Harry Carey in *The Flaming Forties* (Pathé, 1925), one of several versions of Bret Harte's *Tennessee's Partner*

one of the best of the group, is the only program Western that has constantly been included in Western retrospectives arranged by such cultural bodies as New York's Lincoln Center, the George Eastman House in Rochester, Montreal's Cinemathèque Canadienne, and the Venice Film Festival.

Almost as elaborate as the Maynards were the historical Westerns that Tim McCoy made for MGM. McCoy, a military man and an authority on Indian lore and history, was introduced to the movies via *The Covered Wagon.* His job had been to represent and work with the many Indians employed in the film and to accompany them to Europe on publicity work for the film. Reputedly he also did some of the trick riding in the film, although there is precious little of it, and none that couldn't have been performed by any competent wrangler. Paramount later put him into a key supporting role in one of its Zane Grey Westerns, *The Thundering Herd,* but didn't develop him as a Western star. They hadn't retained a regular Western star on the lot since easing William S. Hart out the year before, and for their Zane Grey and other Westerns, they used such contract stars as Neil Hamilton, Antonio Moreno and Jack Holt, and later, Gary Cooper and Lane Chandler. MGM, which made few "B" pictures, and never at any other time in its history sponsored a continuing series of Westerns, launched McCoy in a group of actioners based on various aspects of American history, including events in the Far East and the campaign against the Seminoles in Florida, but with the main emphasis on Western themes. The films, though produced on a big scale, were surprisingly short, some running less than an hour. Their purpose was manifold. They provided second features for Metro's own "A" product in the limited but growing double-feature market; they were useful training grounds for new directors; and at times they were even used to discipline temperamental stars whom the front office thought were getting delusions of grandeur. For example, after playing leads in important major releases, Joan Crawford was taken down a peg or two by being installed as Tim McCoy's leading lady in *Winners of the Wilderness* and *Law of the Range* in 1927 and 1928 respectively. The directors on the McCoy films included William Nigh, the Russian Tourjansky, and W. S. Van Dyke, who, with his outstanding cameraman Clyde de Vinna, more than proved his mettle by jumping from the McCoy westerns to the classic *White Shadows in the South Seas.* Incidentally, Van Dyke's assistant at the time was Lesley Selander, who, in the thirties and forties, became one of the ablest directors of the Buck Jones and Hopalong Cassidy Westerns before moving on to bigger-scale horse operas.

McCoy was a good actor and a striking figure of a man who wore both cowboy costumes and military uniforms with flair. While he was husky and a fine rider, he was always believed that story mattered more than action, and in any case he exuded a natural dignity which somehow made it seem inappropriate for him to engage in fist fights or flying leaps into the saddle. Except for a brief early period in Columbia sound Westerns, McCoy's films usually contained less action than those of any other major Western star, and he also used doubles far more liberally. Despite their often quite spectacular action climaxes and their brief running times, the McCoy Westerns at MGM were not markedly popular with the youngsters (historical data was often documented at some length, and the romantic elements were more dominant than usual) nor were they specifically tailored to the juvenile market. As a footnote without further comment, the MGM product of the late twenties displayed a rather surprising penchant for male nudity in situations of bondage and torture—ranging from the trussed-up galley slave in *Ben Hur* to a writhing victim burning at the stake in at least one of the McCoys. Admittedly, such scenes were discreetly photographed from the rear, but whatever segment of the moviegoing public they were aimed at, it was definitely not the kiddie trade!

One of the most durable of all the new Western stars of the twenties was Buck Jones, who starred for Fox in a series secondary in importance to their Mix films, but hardly secondary in the care with which they were made. Jones struck a neat balance between the conviction of Hart and the excitement of Mix; his films had sensible stories and good if not flamboyant action, and one additional ingredient—an unstressed but definite element of folksy Will Rogers humor. This may well have been a quality that Jones devised himself; gestures and bits of comedy business that he used in such early films as *Just Pals* (directed by John Ford in 1920) he retained and developed through the years. When he was solely in charge of his own productions (in the thirties) he often overdid these comedy elements (primarily because he was a serious actor, one of the best among Western stars, and comic by-play from him too frequently seemed forced when it should have been totally relaxed). Over his more than twenty years of stardom, Jones maintained a remarkably high standard, and he was also the *only* silent Western star who continued over into talkies without once having to descend to independent quickies.

Another star who, like Jones, retained a certain allegiance to the Hart image was Harry Carey. His always mature features, and the fact that he was an actor before he was an athlete, probably made his

Philo McCullough, Hoot Gibson and Ena Gregory in *Calgary Stampede* (Universal, 1925)

Fred Thomson in *Ridin' the Wind* (FBO, 1925)

91

Owen Moore and Constance Bennett in *Code of the West* (Paramount, 1925)

A Hoot Gibson Universal crew on location near the Mexican border: to his right is leading Thelma Percy, and to her right director Mack V. Wright

Examples of the trick riding that characterized Ken Maynard's excellent new series (1926-29) for First National

allegiance unavoidable. In his plots, too, he followed the Hart tradition: in *The Prairie Pirate* he turned good outlaw to track down the murderer of his sister, while *Satan Town* was a vigorous reworking of one of Hart's best pictures, *Hell's Hinges*. None of the Westerns that Carey made after he left John Ford were truly outstanding, but they were enjoyable, intelligent, and well above average programmers. He too continued into the talkies, first as a star of serials and independent Westerns, and then as a character player.

Of the lesser silent Western stars, Leo Maloney and Yakima Canutt were among the more interesting. Leo was a genial star in the Jack Hoxie manner, who formed a writing-producing-directing partnership with Ford Beebe, one of the best directors of slick talkie "B" Westerns and serials. They made some good two-reelers and a few features together, and Maloney enjoyed a large following which could have built him into a top-ranking star had he knuckled down to it. But he was never too serious about making movies, would go off on spur-of-the-moment sprees during shooting, and his films

Señor Daredevil (1926), first of the Maynards for First National

94

often had to be constructed so that the plots allowed him to be absent a great deal of the time. With an off-screen hero, their action content was never pronounced, and hurried script sessions often resulted in the desperate pilfering of plots and situations from other stars' movies. (The entire climax of Hart's *Square Deal Sanderson*—a rather unusual and easily recognizable sequence—was borrowed in this way!)

Canutt likewise never realized his full potential in silent Westerns, though for different reasons. Probably the finest all-around stuntman the screen has ever had,

he tried to make Westerns in the Mix manner, but unfortunately was limited to the cheaper independent companies like Goodwill Productions, who could never provide the budgets necessary for sustained and elaborate stunt sequences. Canutt's Westerns on the whole were slow and poorly directed, but enlivened by frequent leaps, falls, and other horse stunt work. Occasionally the climactic chases would be prolonged far beyond their worth in order to provide a solid reel of Canutt stunting, but it was obvious, repetitious stuff. Canutt's only really worthwhile silent Western was *The*

Devil Horse, a large-scale programmer with excellent mass action as well as individual stunting, and some superior photography of excellent locations. (George Stevens was the film's second cameraman.) Canutt came into his own in the talkie period, first as a stuntman/villain in scores of Westerns for Monogram and Republic, and later as a director and organizer of mass action sequences, reaching far out of the Western field to such films as *Ben Hur.*

FBO, which—after the Ken Maynards at First National—made the best Westerns of the late twenties, was an independent company formed by Joseph P. Kennedy and dedicated almost solely to the making of expert action pictures. These included the stunt thrillers of Richard Talmadge, but Westerns predominated. Tom Mix was with them briefly, after he had left Fox, and Fred Thomson had left FBO to go to Paramount. Their other Western stars: Bob Custer (enjoying a brief popularity not duplicated in the sound period), Tom Tyler (teamed with a diminutive Frankie Darro), Buzz Barton, the boy stunt rider, and Bob Steele. Slick, well-photographed, full of action, each series with its own distinctive style, the FBO Westerns provided the quality that Republic was to provide in the thirties and early forties.

The Night Cry (Warner Bros., 1926) with Rin Tin Tin

Braveheart (Pathé, 1926):
Frank Hagney,
Rod la Rocque,
Tyrone Power, Sr.

96

The Last Frontier (Pathé, 1926): William Boyd's first Western, with Junior Coghlan

A group of the Bob Custers were dug up by television in the sixties, chopped-up, gagged-up, doctored with jazzed-up sound effects and an obnoxious small boy "voice over" narration, edited down to five-minute segments, and somehow their innate quality still managed to show through.

Unfortunately, all too few of the independent Westerns of the twenties matched the quality of the FBO work. The market for double-bills was growing, Westerns were popular, and they were still the cheapest kind of film to make. And since they didn't have to worry about even semi-literate dialogue, clean photography and fast-action were all that they had to worry about. With such simple aims, it is amazing how often they failed to deliver the goods. Indian "uprisings" would consist of a few scraggly extras emerging from two or three tepees; fights were badly staged; the simple plots were prolonged through the excessive use of dialogue titles. Or if a producer like Anthony J. Xydias tried to offer a little more in terms of plot and production trimmings, then the budget wouldn't allow for action too. Xydias made a series of "historical epics" for his Sunset Productions with relatively non-formula plots, casts that included such respectable names as Bryant Washburn

Galloping Jinx (Artclass, 1926): Bud Osborne, Buddy Roosevelt

The Galloping Cowboy (Associated Exhibitors, 1926) with Bill Cody

Open Range (Paramount, 1927) with Betty Bronson, Lane Chandler

and Bob Steele, capable directors like Robert N. Bradbury (Bob Steele's father), and lengths that, by virtue of being a reel or two over the average "B" product, suggested that maybe these films were in fact "outdoor epics" and not just "Westerns." While they were pleasant enough and certainly not the mental and physical wastelands offered by Al Hoxie in *The Ace of Clubs* and Dick Hatton in *Pioneer Days,* they were still basically "cheaters." After all, it is a little disconcerting to be lured into a theatre to see *With Sitting Bull at the Spirit Lake Massacre* only to find in reel six that the slaughter has taken place off-screen!

With so many top-quality Westerns on the market, it is hard to understand how the cheaters could survive. Why should anyone book a non-action Western with a nonentity as star when for a few dollars more he could get a crowd-pleasing Tom Tyler—or for a slightly higher price, play a Tom Mix that would undoubtedly outgross John Barrymore's *When a Man Loves?* The answer, of course, is that the cheaters didn't really survive for long. They got only nominal bookings, but their costs were so low that they needed relatively few bookings to show a profit. Exhibitors, on the other hand, finding that a given producer turned out junk and that their audiences

Winners of the Wilderness (MGM, 1927) with Tim McCoy, Chief White Horse

Nevada (Paramount, 1927): Gary Cooper (mounted) and William Powell

The Arizona Whirlwind
(Pathé, 1927) with
Bill Cody

The Grey Devil (Rayart, 1927) with Jack Perrin

Drums of the Desert (Paramount 1927) with Warner Baxter and Marietta Milner

The Denver Dude (Universal, 1927) Hoot Gibson and Rolfe Sedan

Arizona Bound (Paramount, 1927) with Gary Cooper, Jack Daugherty

California (MGM, 1927) with Tim McCoy, Dorothy Sebastien, Roy D'Arcy

White Gold (Pathé, 1927), directed by William K. Howard, with George Bancroft, Jetta Goudal, Kenneth Thomson

were voluble in their dislike for a certain Western star would give that producer and that star the cold shoulder when the next booking season came around. By then, another fly-by-night outfit would have appeared on the horizon, and it too would be given a chance for a season of unimportant one-day, bottom of the bill bookings. The producers came and went, the lesser stars, devoid of acting or athletic ability, often not even possessed of personality or a pleasant face, enjoyed their brief moment of stardom, and vanished. The independent silent field contained more writers who couldn't write, actors who couldn't act, comedians who couldn't raise a laugh, and Western stars without get-up-and-go than has ever before or since been concentrated in any part of the movie or television industry. Indeed, it is hard to think of any industry, let alone art, in which so much mediocrity was carried along, if only temporarily, by the momentum of quality of the rest of that industry.

But in the late twenties the movies had far more to worry about than the malingerers and cheaters in their midst. 1925 had seemed like a bad year, with attendance falling off due to the competition of "free" home entertainment—radio. A rush of good pictures had licked that crisis. The sudden popularity of German pictures,

Pioneer Scout (Paramount, 1928) with Fred Thomson, Nora Lane

The Wind (MGM, 1928), directed by Victor Seastrom: Lars Hanson and Lillian Gish

and the birth of the "art-house" idea, overnight made it fashionable for Hollywood to import German directors and stars and for Hollywood film-makers to inject as much German "technique" into their films as possible. Unexpectedly, the Western managed to absorb some of this technique rather effectively. A humble Jack Perrin Western for Universal, *Wild Blood,* was directed by that old Western and serial maestro Henry MacRae. Yet visually it was right out of *Warning Shadows,* with much moving camera work, symbolism, trick effects, and even a wild hallucination sequence for the heroine, all in the midst of an ultra-traditional action story.

Even more notable was *White Gold,* one of the forgotten classics of the silents, all the more remarkable in that it was directed by William K. Howard, a man always notable for pace and dazzling photographic technique, but a specialist in action and melodrama rather than psychology. (He had directed some of the best Zane Grey Westerns for Paramount.) Yet *White Gold* was a slow-moving, deliberately claustrophobic story with only two sets, five characters, and no physical action at all. It dealt in such intangibles as jealousy, envy and frustration, and handed the audience at least two big shocks. One was the killing off of the "hero"

(George Bancroft) quite casually and unexpectedly; the other was a deliberately ambiguous climax in which the audience had to make up its own mind as to what *had* happened and what was *going* to happen. Audiences in those pre-Godard and Resnais days, were not used to being forced to involve themselves emotionally in films. *White Gold* was a big critical success, being compared favorably with such German films as *The Last Laugh,* and while not a bonanza at the box office, it must have been so economical to make that no great loss could have been incurred. *White Gold* tended to be overlooked and forgotten when, a year later (1928), MGM made a very similar film in *The Wind.* Certainly *The Wind* is a better film; subtler, more cinematically directed by the Swedish Victor Seastrom, graced by a brilliant and vibrant performance from Lillian Gish. But *White Gold* (its title refers to wool, the story taking place on a sheep ranch) came first, and may well have been the inspiration for the making of *The Wind.* In any event, it was the most notable psychological Western until the arrival of *The Ox-Bow Incident* and *The Gunfighter* two decades later.

By the end of the twenties, the Western was at its lowest ebb since the days immediately prior to William

Shooting an action sequence with a crew of four, extra players, and Fred Thomson, for *Jesse James* (Paramount, 1928)

S. Hart. The epic had all but vanished from the screen and the movies were going through a curious period in which the big Northern action story *(The Trail of 98, The Michigan Kid, Tide of Empire)* was enjoying a huge vogue, while the Western was being relegated more and more to a less important budgetary area. The arrival of talkies brought with it both technical problems (especially where location shooting was concerned) and the commercial need to exploit dialogue for its own sake. A further if less expected handicap to the Western's survival was Lindbergh's epochal flight across the Atlantic. Overnight the nation, and especially the youth of the nation, became aviation-conscious. *Photoplay* magazine editorialized in April of 1929:

"Lindbergh has put the cowboy into the discard . . . the Western novel and motion picture heroes have slunk away into the brush, never to return. The cow ponies are retired to the pasture with the old fire horses. Tom Mix, Hoot Gibson, and Ken Maynard must swap horses for airplanes or go to the old actors' home."

Vivid action scenes from *California Mail* (First National, 1929); seventeenth in the Maynard series, with no lessening of quality

THE COMING OF SOUND

It would seem that the Western, telling its story in terms of action rather than dialogue, should have been relatively unconcerned about the mechanical problems of sound. The mystery film and the sophisticated comedy were forced to tell their stories via dialogue, and in order not to seem impossibly stagey and static they *needed* camera movement and as much of the film grammar of the silents as could be salvaged. For the most part, they didn't get it. Because of many actual and alleged problems, including most specifically the recording of the camera's own operational noise, the cameras became rooted to the ground and housed in small "sweat boxes." For a year or two, the cinema duplicated the stage; dialogue was king, and filmic style was thrown out of

the window. Of course, the good directors—the Vidors and the Mamoulians and the Fords—insisted on maintaining a fluid camera and on trying for dramatic weldings of sound and image. Enough good and thoroughly cinematic films were still made in the years 1929-31 to confound the pat claims by "historians" that the film came to a dead halt in these years and had to learn to be an art all over again.

But achieving this artistry and combatting the claims of cameramen and efficiency experts that such-and-such just couldn't be done meant time, sweat and mechanical know-how. In the first year or two of sound, the Western didn't seem important enough to justify this kind of effort. Like the big elaborate swashbuckler, it was considered a dead relic of the silents and of no major commercial value. MGM scrapped its elaborate Tim McCoy series entirely. FBO, undergoing corporate and operational changes that turned it first into RKO-Pathé and later RKO Radio, likewise abandoned its program Westerns, and with them Tom Mix. (They would resume in a year or two with a Tom Keene series, and thereafter retain a regular "B" Western series until the early fifties). Warner Brothers, also in doubt about the commercial value of Westerns, jettisoned their "B" Westerns too. Of all the major companies, only Universal, geared to "little" pictures and programmers far more than the other big companies, carried its silent cowboy heroes, Hoot Gibson and Ken Maynard, over into talkies. Gibson's slow-paced format and his stress on comedy and plot rather than action made him an early casualty of sound Westerns as a major star. He was soon, and for the rest of his career, working only for the smaller independent companies. Universal, recognizing that it had to offer talkie Westerns or lose out on the new market, but also wanting to service the slow-dying remnants of the silent market, and reluctant to spend extra money on what it felt was still an unimportant product, came up with a kind of compromise. Once or twice in each film, the plot would stop dead for a long dialogue-expository sequence which would satisfy those demanding talkies, and which could easily be shortened and titled for the silent version. (In *Lucky Larkin* it took place in a long, box-like saloon.) Their ten-episode Tim McCoy serial, full of elaborate moving camerawork, likewise contained one extremely static dialogue sequence in each episode, while the last chapter, as a kind of bonus, disposed of its wrap-up action almost immediately and devoted the bulk of its footage to a long conversation between the hero and the heroine, in which he describes his pal's apparent death—only to have the pal (Edmund Cobb) turn up alive and kicking as an excuse for more 100% all-talking explanations and rejoicings!

Fortunately the stalemate of the hybrid part-talkie Western solved itself very quickly. In 1929, Raoul Walsh made *In Old Arizona* for Fox, a Cisco Kid Western starring Warner Baxter that was hardly a super-Western but was certainly one of style and importance. Microphones hidden under prairie scrub and foliage enabled naturalistic sound effects to be picked up, and even more than the gunshots and the galloping hooves, the sound of frying bacon impressed itself on viewers and showed that the realistic quality of sound was perhaps just what the Western needed.

The Virginian (Paramount, 1929), directed by Victor Fleming; Gary Cooper and Walter Huston

At this time the studios were again experimenting with the oft-tried and abandoned idea of wide-screen projection—a curiously ambitious and ill-timed experiment, since the more practical and commercial experiments with sound and color still had a great many bugs to be ironed out. Obviously the Western was an ideal testing ground for the Giant-Screen movie, and two major ones were produced in 70mm, although after a few showcase runs they were generally distributed in the standard 35mm gauge. The first of these was *The Big Trail,* again directed by Raoul Walsh for Fox, and giving John Wayne his first starring role. In terms of size and action, it is still one of the most impressive of all super-Westerns. (Its German version, made simultaneously, was still playing commercially in German theatres in the post-World War II period, and its big Indian battle scenes were used continually through the thirties and forties to pad out cheaper pictures.) The detailing of the assembly of the covered wagon train, its departure from the midwest, the agonizingly real scenes showing the train fording a swollen river in a storm, and the dismantling of the wagons so that they could be hauled over mountains carried far more drama and conviction than anything in *The Covered Wagon.* And its tradi-

Technical advisor William S. Hart hands Johnny Mack Brown one of Billy the Kid's own guns; *Billy the Kid* (1930)

Billy the Kid (MGM, 1930), directed by King Vidor; with Wallace Beery, Johnny Mack Brown

110

Hell's Heroes (Universal, 1930), directed by William Wyler; Fritzie Ridgeway, Charles Bickford, Walter James

tional Indian battle—hordes of savages surrounding the huge circle of wagons—is still the most spectacular such sequence ever filmed. A buffalo hunt sequence also carried complete conviction, with genuine riding closeups of the players replacing the phony mock-ups of *The Covered Wagon.* All of this, slammed over with Walsh's customary virility and pace, and composed with its widescreen effect very much in mind, made *The Big Trail* an outstanding early sound epic. So authentic did it look that just a few years ago a Kansas historical foundation, coming across some glass negatives of the wagon train assembly and departure sequence, understandably waxed loud and long in their excitement at having found rare original photographic coverage of the actual event! But, as with *The Iron Horse,* the authenticity of detail and the sweep of history was somewhat let down by a standardized "B" plot, hinging around the hero's search for the murderer of his brother. Moreover, John Wayne's inexperience was thrown into sharp relief by all the veteran players in the cast, and El Brendel's comedy was another cliché intrusion.

King Vidor's *Billy the Kid,* made in 1930 for MGM, was a better picture in many ways, but a slower one, and certainly a smaller-scale and less commercial one. Photographed largely on the actual locations of the famous Lincoln County wars, it was again carefully composed with the giant screen in mind. There were superb panoramic shots and intricate use of terrain and natural lighting—as in a sequence where Billy is besieged in a cave among colorful rock formations, while Sheriff Pat Garrett, below, entices him out of hiding (by frying more bacon!). In fact, the whole film was so carefully composed for wide screen projection that, encountering the same problems as the early CinemaScope films, it avoided closeups entirely. When seen on a normal sized screen, this concentration on long shots and two-shots gave it a stilted and almost primitive quality. It was already a rather old-fashioned film; like most early talkies, it had no musical score and one was sorely needed, if only for punctuation in the transitional scenes. In lieu of music, silent-style subtitles were employed to bridge dramatic gaps and time lapses. Moreover, director Vidor deliberately tried to avoid the traditional MGM gloss; the photography is good, but always naturalistic, the characters drab in their dress, the buildings ramshackle, the streets dusty. It is a long film and a slow one, with its main action sequence placed in the middle of the film, so that it doesn't even build to a climax as most Westerns do. Its script is frankly untidy, yet the film is quite certainly the best

111

and most convincing of all the Billy the Kid sagas.

Johnny Mack Brown, later to be a leading star of "B" Westerns, but prior to this known mainly as a clothes-horse society leading man to Greta Garbo, Mary Pickford and Joan Crawford, brought athletic ability and a pleasing personality to the role of Billy, although it was Wallace Beery as Pat Garrett who gave the best performance, a surprisingly underplayed piece of acting for such an extrovert player and an equally surprisingly underwritten role. In *Billy the Kid* Vidor created the first of the only two sound Westerns (the second was *Law and Order* in 1932) to really recapture the rugged austerity of the silent Bill Hart Westerns. Possibly his own creative efforts may have been helped along by the difficulties inherent in shooting such a talkative Western away from the easier conditions of the studio, difficulties that may have occasionally given the film an even rougher-hewn quality than Vidor really wanted. No doubt much of the film's effortless authenticity can be attributed to the fact that Hart worked on the film as an advisor, coached Brown, and even lent him Billy's own six-guns. Hart must surely have been dismayed, however, by the tacked-on happy ending in which the benign Garrett instead of shooting Billy down sends him over the border to safety and a peaceful life with his sweetheart. A romanticized (but closer to the facts) ending, in which Billy is shot by Garrett and dies in his arms, was filmed, but retained only for the European versions.

Production crew shooting *The Spoilers* (Paramount, 1930), third of the five versions to date

Since Billy's various killings are shown as being decidedly cold-blooded, even if somewhat justified by circumstance, the sudden happy-ever-after ending is a little hard to accept.

Although the wide-screen was well-utilized in *The Big Trail* and *Billy the Kid*, enthusiasm for it did not last. Before its quick demise, it was already being used only as a gimmick to prop up weak pictures, as in *The Lash*, a rather pedestrian Western starring Richard Barthelmess, in which only a large-scale cattle stampede sequence could in any way be said to justify the big screen. Oddly enough, the two-color Technicolor process, then enjoying a big vogue, and the many competitive lesser color processes, were not harnessed at this time to the big-scale Western. Color was reserved largely for musicals and only saw service in the great outdoors when the film in question was, like *Rio Rita*, essentially a musical that happened also to have a Western locale. By the time that *Cimarron*, the third big Western epic of the sound era, arrived in 1931, the big screen was all but forgotten. *Cimarron*, commercially the "safest" of the three in that it was based on a best-selling novel by Edna Ferber, was probably the best film of its versatile but not very imaginative director, Wesley Ruggles. Like his later *Arizona*, it tended to be bogged down in character studies and had the structural flaw of presenting its highlight—the massive Cherokee Strip landrush sequence—at the beginning of the picture. Thereafter, its

The Spoilers (1930)

typically sprawling Ferber canvas depicted the growth and development of Oklahoma as an oil-rich state over the years more in terms of emotion and heartbreak than in visual excitement. Nevertheless, the film was well served by Richard Dix and Irene Dunne in the leads, many good supporting performances, and by opening reels so strong (not only in physical action, but in the convincing depiction of the construction of the frontier town) that their impetus carried the film through its later, more pedestrian segments.

A big commercial success, *Cimarron* prompted not so much a series of further Western epics, as a number of outright imitations using the same *Cavalcade* formula of a young couple coming West, raising a family, participating in the opening up of new territories, and bringing them through financial crises and political turmoil to the early thirties, when the spoiled, easy-living activities of their children cried out for a return to the pioneer spirit to lift America from the doldrums of the Depression.

The Mary Pickford-Leslie Howard film *Secrets*, directed by Frank Borzage, was an interesting film in this group, stronger on emotional qualities than on Western action, and with some of its biggest scenes lifted bodily from *The Covered Wagon.* Rather better and preceding it by a year, was 1932's *The Conquerors,* an obvious attempt (but a good one) by RKO Radio to repeat the success of *Cimarron,* even to starring Richard Dix again. Directed by William Wellman, it contained some unusually powerful sequences, including the death of the family's son in an accident as the crowds are lined up to welcome the first locomotive and a grim mass lynching episode so starkly designed and lit, and so casually underplayed, that it quite outshines the more carefully and lengthily constructed lynching scenes in Wellman's much later *The Ox-Bow Incident.*

1932 also saw the production of another of the sound era's most overlooked Westerns (and one of its finest) *Law and Order.* Although based on a novel by W. R. Burnett, using fictional names, it was clearly built around the lives of Wyatt Earp (played by Walter Huston) and

The Big Trail (Fox, 1930), directed by Raoul Walsh, starring John Wayne. The realism of this classic early sound epic shows through quite clearly in these stills.

The Big Trail

Doc Holiday (Harry Carey). Its director was Edward Cahn, who had just completed an apprenticeship under arty director Paul Fejos and was anxious to show what he could do. His directorial debut was also his artistic zenith; he never again made a film one-tenth as good. *Law and Order,* partially scripted by John Huston, was a slow-paced, gritty Western that matched *Billy the Kid* in recapturing the old Ince-Hart flavor. There was a great deal of tension, but little traditional physical action throughout the bulk of the film, which literally exploded in its last reel into the finest reconstruction yet of the famous gun duel at the O.K. Corral. Influenced no doubt by Fejos, who had always been a specialist in elaborately fluid use of the moving camera, Cahn made his camera a participant in the short, sharp, tightly edited battle, darting from side to side in subjective viewpoints, catching the sudden terror of a frightened horse.

Perhaps the real beauty of *Law and Order* lay in its formal yet unforced style. At the end, the Marshal, sole survivor of the battle, rides out of town weary of killing, yet knowing that more such towns await him and his guns; the compositions, stressing his feeling of isolation; the mournful tolling of the church bell; the citizens glad to have the job done but unwilling to have involved

themselves in it; all of this achieved a sense of Greek tragedy without consciously striving for it (as *High Noon* was to do). *Law and Order* was remade twice, once as a formula Johnny Mack Brown "B" in the forties, and again as a Technicolor action-filled and somewhat brutal Ronald Reagon "A" in the fifties. The original film had no women in it at all, other than for the brief appearance of a dowdy saloon trollop. The second remake had *two* leading ladies, and a great deal of sex and bedroom suggestiveness. One of the finest and most poignant episodes in the original was a touching and sensitive sequence in which the lawmen are forced to hang a simple-minded, good-hearted farm lad (Andy Devine) who had become an accidental murderer, a sub-plot that effectively stressed that problems of morality and conscience could confuse and deter the early lawmen just as much as a confrontation with outnumbering enemy forces. In the remake, this genuinely classic sequence was distorted into a standard lynching by the villains.

Perhaps the very starkness of Westerns like *Law and Order* mitigated against their success. After all, by 1932, the movies had really solved all of the technical problems connected with sound and were entering into their greatest period of lush, smooth, glossy glamor. 1932

118

was the year of Lubitsch's silken *Trouble in Paradise,* the all-star paean to elegance *Grand Hotel,* and Mamoulian's sparkling *Love Me Tonight.* Audiences wanted escape from Depression problems, and Westerns like *Billy the Kid* and *Law and Order* didn't provide that escape. They showed, far more graphically than most later Westerns, that a bullet in the stomach really hurt, and that dying of thirst and hunger in the desert was just as much a part of the "glorious" West as leading a spectacular Cavalry charge against the Apaches. Most of the other "A" Westerns—not that there were many of them—tended to reflect this rather downbeat attitude. Or, like *The Painted Desert,* they remembered too determinedly that they were "talkies" and told too much of their stories in words rather than deeds. *The Painted Desert,* however, was partially redeemed by the dynamic presence of Clark Gable, playing his first major role as the villain with such force and animal magnetism that he stole the film away from the placid and stereotyped heroics of William Boyd.

But for the real excitement and action of the Western,

audiences turned to the "B" pictures. By 1932, most of the big silent Western heroes were re-established in series of their own: Tom Mix, Buck Jones, Tim McCoy, George O'Brien, Ken Maynard. The independent producers, cashing in on a greatly expanded double-bill market, embarked on the prolific mass production of scores of cheap Westerns, employing not only the lesser stars of the silents (Bob Custer, Bill Cody, Jack Perrin) but those bigger stars (Hoot Gibson, Bob Steele, Tom Tyler, Jack Hoxie) who were unable to find more imposing berths in the now restricted Western output of the bigger studios. And to the imposing list of veterans, interesting new stars were added: John Wayne at Warners, Tom Keene at RKO. It was the beginning of the movies' biggest boom in grade "B" horse operas, a boom that would last at peak level for nearly fifteen years, a veritable paradise for the Western fans who cared nothing (or very little) for the poetry of Ford or the realism of Hart, but loved the non-stop sound of galloping hooves, crackling six-guns, and the impact of fist on chin.

The Big Trail

The Great Meadow (MGM, 1931): Johnny Mack Brown, Eleanor Boardman

The Conquering Horde (Paramount, 1931): Richard Arlen, Fay Wray

The Painted Desert (Pathé, 1931): Helen Twelvetrees, J. Farrell MacDonald, Clark Gable

Cimarron (RKO Radio, 1931), directed by Wesley Ruggles; the Cherokee Strip landrush

Caught (Paramount, 1931):
Richard Arlen, and Louise
Dresser as Calamity Jane

Cimarron: Richard Dix and
William Collier, Jr.

Cimarron (RKO Radio,
1931), directed by
Wesley Ruggles; the
Cherokee Strip landrush

122

Law and Order
(Universal, 1932), directed
by Edward Cahn;
Walter Huston, Raymond
Hatton, Andy Devine,
Harry Carey, Russell Hopton

THE "B" BOOM

The new medium of talkies proved a great leveller, and the "B" Westerns of independents and major companies alike started out on a relatively even basis. Westerns could still be made cheaply, and the smaller companies as yet had no need to practice the economies that in due time would help to distinguish them from their big studio counterparts. The independents could still afford enough extras so that crowd scenes didn't appear skimpy, and a camera car was not yet a luxury, so even the cheaper Westerns indulged in that ultimate finesse, the running insert or riding closeup. Shooting two or three Westerns at the same time justified the expense of going to worthwhile locations. The one big deficiency of all early "B" Westerns was the lack of a musical score, and exciting *agitato* themes were an absolute essential to the genre, often literally making the difference between a gripping Western and a dull one. In the early sound period, however, musical scores were suspect and considered totally artificial in the new "realistic" medium of talkies. Original scores for movies came into vogue around 1932, and were an additional and considerable expense. The economy-minded independents were reluctant to pay for what seemed a luxury, and this, probably more than any other single factor, is what eventually gave "class" to the major studio "B" Westerns, and denied it to many of the independents.

But prior to this division, both brands of Westerns shared the same physical "look" and the same drawbacks. Action sequences in the early talkies were often shot silent, and even filmed at the old silent speed, to give them a frenzied and speeded-up look when intercut with the dialogue and other sound sequences. While the major studios had their own standing sets and Western streets, the independents, often with no studios of their own, had to rent their ranch and Western street locales, or go to locations where relics of the real thing still existed. These small, often shabby concentrations of wooden shacks invariably looked far more convincing than the big studio reconstructions and injected a surprising amount of unsought-for realism. In one other way, too, the independents often had a striking if unwitting advantage over the majors. Anxious to turn out program Westerns that looked expensive but were still cheap to make, the bigger companies frequently built entire series around the spectacular highlights of their silent Westerns. Thus John Wayne's series at Warner Brothers was carefully patterned after the silent Ken Maynard series, using both basic plots and extensive chunks of action material. A few new chase scenes and a fight or two added to the old and very big-scale highlights made them fast-paced and actionful indeed, but story values suffered badly, and there were many unavoidable restrictions. For matching-up purposes, Wayne had to dress like Maynard, wear the same kind of clothes, ride the same kind of horse, surround himself with the same kind of sidekicks. Either the old plots were followed scrupulously, which meant a lot of padded and extraneous dialogue sequences, or a new plot was written, and then absurd twists or quick explanatory lines of dialogue had to be introduced in order to pave the way for the utilization of stock sequences. Big films and small, right through the fifties, continued to follow this practice of making new films out of old. Not one of them ever had any real merit on its own, no matter how actionful it may have been, or how fascinating to the more studious viewer identifying all the clips used.

The independents, on the other hand, with no such vast reserve of stock material to call on, had to concentrate on story as much as action, and because of this, many of the early independent Westerns had scripts far superior to those of the bigger studios. An early World-Wide Western such as *Riders of the Desert,* a Bob Steele vehicle, not only boasted superior photography, good locations, and some excellent action sequences, but a really strong plot-line as well. Superior scripts continued to be a hallmark of many of the independent Westerns of the early thirties. *Law of the 45's,* a Big Boy Williams Western based on a William Colt MacDonald story,

Buck Jones

Tim McCoy

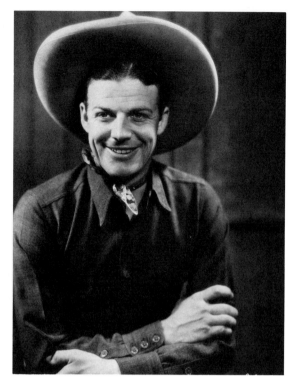

Rex Bell

Kermit Maynard (brother of Ken, a good actor, superb rider, and star of an above-average independent series)

William Boyd

Gene Autry and Champion

Charles Starrett

Bill Elliott

Jack Randall

Bob Baker

The Three Mesquiteers:
Max Terhune,
Bob Livingston,
Ray Corrigan

stressed mystery rather than action, with appropriate atmospheric lighting to back it up. In *Arizona Badman*, Edmund Cobb's sympathetic good-badman characterization in the old Hart tradition, was given far more prominence than the standard heroics of nominal star Reb Russell. And *Toll of the Desert* included an episode worthy of Zane Grey, wherein the apparently orphaned hero grows to manhood and a sheriff's post, and unknowingly executes his own outlaw father on the gallows!

Few independent series of the mid-thirties matched the (relative) quality of a good Kermit Maynard series produced by Ambassador Films. Simple but adequate in their plots, they did at least offer a certain polish in their utilization of effective musical scores, camera trucks for running inserts, elaborate opticals and dissolves, and other technical niceties usually denied the cheaper "B." Moreover they were generously supplied with action and had a big asset in star Kermit Maynard, who was possessed of a breezy, naturalistic acting style and was an accomplished stuntman and rider. He was actually a far better actor than brother Ken, but never had the opportunity to match his popularity.

But the "quality" independents grew fewer as the thirties wore on. Such films were sold in groups and brought in a fairly fixed income regardless of quality, so

George O'Brien

The Utah Kid (Tiffany, 1930)
Tom Santschi,
Boris Karloff,
Lafe McKee

Man from Death Valley (Monogram, 1931): Tom Tyler,
Stanley Blystone

there was little incentive to turn out a better product. The Westerns that aimed at a modicum of quality via either strong stories or an above-average star (Conway Tearle, a dramatic actor, was starred in one series) spent their money in that direction and had little left over for location work or action. Or if action was the desired quality, as in the cheapies from Resolute and similar companies, then a maximum of poorly staged fights and chases, constant use of stock footage, and a total lack of finesse were the modus operandi. These really cheap independent Westerns were often shot in two or three days for a total negative cost well below $10,000, and every dollar that wasn't spent showed up on the screen. Retakes were unheard of, and if an actor fluffed a line or leaped into the saddle and missed, then the flawed scenes were left in. Frequently one could pick up the voice of the director giving instructions, and a quickie with Buffalo Bill, Jr., entitled *Lightning Bill* offered a number of unique illustrations of this kind of slaplash production. The camera frequently picked up the ill-concealed mattresses onto which riders made their falls as they were shot from the saddle, and in one gun battle sequence, a production assistant, thinking that the scene is over, ambles out from behind a tree. Seeing that the cameras are still grinding, he jumps back into cover again—and then, some seconds later, convinced that by now the take must be over, furtively creeps forth again, only to retreat for a second time. However, perhaps the crowning indignity of this particular film was that even its main title was misspelled!

The calibre of the independent Westerns picked up spectacularly, however, with the formation of two "in-between" companies, Monogram and Republic. Both aimed at a "bread-and-butter" product, but they had their own studios, contract writers and directors, and used good veteran stars as well as developing new ones. Republic was at its peak in the late thirties and very early forties. Monogram, while never reaching Republic standards, did turn out many excellent Westerns. At their peak, both companies made some of the best Westerns on the market, and at all times they were well above the quickie level and able to compete favorably with the current product from the major companies.

As the thirties began, the best "B" Westerns were being turned out, rather surprisingly, by the still quite young company, Columbia. They had two of the best Western stars of all, Buck Jones and Tim McCoy, making simultaneous series, and (an unexpected bonus years later, when the films hit television) a young John Wayne had supporting roles in several of them. Both McCoy and Jones took their Westerns seriously, and gave them

such care and variety of plot that none of them had an assembly-line look to them. Both alternated purely action Westerns with those in which plot took the dominant role. McCoy's *The Riding Tornado* was all-action stuff that lived up to its title, but conversely *The End of the Trail* was a slow, methodical, obviously sincere and sometimes genuinely poetic study of the white man's betrayal of the Indian. There was no villain in the normal sense and a rather surprising element of tragedy; McCoy's young son is killed by the cavalry, and in the original version, McCoy himself died at the end, though a last-minute happy ending was hastily tacked on before the film went into release. Many of the other McCoys were essentially detective stories, the Western settings almost incidental.

Both series benefitted from solid production values and good directors. Some of the films, such as Jones' *White Eagle,* directed by Lambert Hillyer, turned out so well that in later years they would almost certainly have been separated from their series format and sold as specials. After a few seasons, however, the inevitable lessening of enthusiasm—and budget-cutting—that affects every series Western began to set in. Both the Jones and the McCoy series began to lose lustre. Jones actually left Columbia to go to Universal, then returned to Columbia later with a "modern" series that presented him in such

Near the Trail's End
(Tiffany, 1931),
with Bob Steele

130

The Holy Terror
(Fox, 1931),
with George O'Brien

off-beat roles as a lettuce farmer and a Western star's double.

However, at their peak, both McCoy and Jones produced for Columbia some of the industry's highest quality "B" Westerns, films that could be enjoyed by adults as much as by youngsters. Indeed, many of them were clearly intended for adults. Jones' *The Avenger,* in which he played Mexican bandit Juaquin Murietta, was a rather grim little film played for tension rather than action, and with superb lighting and photography from Charles Stumar, a cameraman not normally associated with Westerns.

Taking over as Columbia's new Western star was Charles Starrett. He was handsome and athletic, but his white Stetson and impeccable dress immediately proclaimed him one of the new breed of "streamlined" Western stars, a far cry from the veterans he was replacing. But the initial Starrett Westerns were good and they got even better, reaching their peak in the late thirties with films like *Two Gun Law*. Thereafter, they rapidly became formularized: the same casts in picture after picture, the same basic plots, a plethora of action, a dearth of originality. Nevertheless, they retained a certain level of quality, declining only in the final years of the "B" Western in the early fifties. Starrett stayed

Branded (Columbia, 1931), with Buck Jones

with Columbia as their No. 1 Western star for almost two decades. The studio also produced a Ken Maynard series, and tried out two straight (if indistinguished) dramatic actors in short-lived series in the late thirties: Jack Luden and Bob Allen.

Far more successful was Gordon Elliott, who had been in movies since the mid-twenties, and who was suddenly introduced as a new Western star in the late thirties. Elliott played in a sober, restrained fashion, clearly modelling his characterization after William S. Hart. He had known Hart and at one time was under consideration to portray him in a movie biography. The initial Elliotts at Columbia were excellent "B"s, espe-

Fox, having lost Buck Jones and Tom Mix at the end of the silents, turned over its Westerns to George O'Brien, now no longer as big a star as he had been in the twenties, but with a following in the action market. O'Brien was goodlooking and muscular, an ex-Naval boxing champ who could more than take care of himself in the fights, and an ex-stuntman who rarely used doubles himself. Moreover, he had an excellent sense of humor, and was particularly good in "taming-of-the-shrew" variations where he was called upon to bait the heroine. His initial films for Fox were important—not major Westerns admittedly, but well above the "B" or programmer level. They had good scripts, many based

My Pal the King (Universal, 1932), with Paul Hurst, Tom Mix, Wallis Clark, Mickey Rooney, and Noel Francis

cially *In Early Arizona*, another unofficial adaptation of the Wyatt Earp story. Elliott also starred in three Western serials which were superior in production values, but almost devoid of story values, degenerating into a repetitive series of unmotivated fights and chases before the ends of the first episodes. After a promising start, the Elliotts declined in quality very quickly, not even matching the more formularized (but at least vigorous) Charles Starrett series. However, Elliott was to regain his lost ground in good later series at Republic and Monogram.

on Zane Grey novels, good directors, and, as with the Mix films, excellent photography and locations. They also served as useful training ground for new stars that Fox was grooming: Humphrey Bogart, George Brent, Maureen O'Sullivan, Myrna Loy. But they were undoubtedly too expensive to compete with the many other "B" Westerns on the market, and were abandoned in the mid-thirties.

O'Brien was shifted into an independent series of much lower quality for Sol Lesser, and released through Fox. However, at least one of these, *When a Man's a*

Man, from the Harold Bell Wright novel, proved to be a genuine "sleeper." Intelligently played (with a particularly strong and likeable performance from Dorothy Wilson as the heroine), and with a logical, literate script, it avoided most of the clichés, built up to an extremely exciting climax, and even had the wit to let its rather reasonable villain (Harry Woods) get away scot-free. One of its greatest assets was the beautifully lit camerawork of one of the most underrated of all cinematographers, Frank Good. *When a Man's a Man* is one of the best "little" Westerns ever made.

Right through the thirties Paramount continued to make (and remake) its highly popular Zane Grey series. At the beginning of the sound period they were still almost "specials"—*Fighting Caravans* with Gary Cooper ran for nine reels. Through the early thirties they decreased in length (many of them running less than an hour) while increasing in quality, but by the end of the thirties there was a tendency for them to creep up to seven- and eight-reel lengths again. Although the average standard was high, they were an uneven group of Westerns, some being so faithful to the original Grey novels that their plot complications and multiplicity of characters worked against them. Others, like *Man of the Forest* and *The Thundering Herd,* were built around footage from the silent versions, a deception that was aided by re-hiring many of the same players so that footage a decade apart could be intercut more easily.

On the whole, however, it was an extremely good series, making excellent use of such contract directors as Henry Hathaway and such contract players as Randolph Scott, Raymond Hatton, Buster Crabbe, Tom Keene, Monte Blue, Noah Beery (a marvelous fruity villain in many of them), and Harry Carey. Within the limits of the "B" framework, many could have been considered models of their kind, especially *To the Last Man* with its strong story of feuding families in the post-Civil War era, and its unusual climactic fight between the villain (Jack LaRue) and the *heroine* (Esther Ralston). One might also mention *Thunder Trail.* Few "B" Westerns ever gave more value for money than it did. A good story, based on *Arizona Ames,* its 58 minutes spanned some fifteen years with its long-lost brother motif, found time for logical writing, subtle characterizations *and* constant action. It was given additional freshness by the use of players not then associated with Westerns: Gilbert Roland as the hero, J. Carrol Naish as his Mexican sidekick, Charles Bickford as the villain, and Marsha Hunt as the heroine. In addition, it was photographed by one of the best cameramen in the business, Karl Struss, and the additional care showed in every foot of film.

In 1935, Paramount initiated a new series, based on Clarence E. Mulford's "Hopalong Cassidy" books. Uncertain at first that the initial film in the series would be popular enough to justify even a few follow-ups, Paramount certainly had no idea that it would develop into one of the most popular Western series of all, sustaining itself until the end of the forties and then switching to television. One of the keys to its success, of course, was the personality of its star, William Boyd, a former De-

A 1932 Paramount publicity shot: William S. Hart helping to "Americanize" Maurice Chevalier

133

End of the Trail (Columbia, 1933), with Lafe McKee, Wheeler
Oakman, Tim McCoy

Man of the Forest (Paramount, 1933), with Randolph Scott,
Noah Beery, Sr., Harry Carey

Breed of the Border (Monogram, 1933), with Bob Steele

Breed of the Border (Monogram, 1933), with Bob Steele,
George Hayes, Marion Byron, Fred Cavens

Robbers' Roost (Fox, 1933), with George O'Brien

Mille player who could command the following of adults as well as children. The screen character created for Cassidy was nothing like Mulford's original; in Boyd's hands he became both a gentleman and a modern cavalier. The scripts occasionally went overboard in rather mawkish sentiment to establish his nobility and the pedestal he was placed on by small boys, hard-pressed widows, and ill-treated dogs. Nevertheless, the Boyd characterization became so popular that when the Mulford novels were later reissued, they were partially rewritten to conform to the "new" Cassidy image.

The first Cassidy Westerns were in many ways the best. They lacked polish, but they had good scripts and casts, and created a realistic picture of ranch life with its humdrum chores and boisterous horseplay. Action was played down at first, partly because the scenarios were thoughtful and reasonably faithful adaptations of specific Mulford novels, partly too because Boyd (who had made only a couple of lesser "A" Westerns before)

was not yet an accomplished action star, and had to be doubled in all of his riding and fights, primarily by Cliff Lyons. The first dozen films, however, made up for their somewhat slow pace by climaxes of astonishing vigor and scope; the build-up would be methodical, and then suddenly these large-scale action climaxes would hit the screen, accompanied by the equally sudden introduction of background music, which had been witheld during earlier, lesser action sequences. The format was an interesting one, and was copied by many other Western producers, but it was also a rigidly restrictive one. Wisely, it was abandoned after it had served its purpose. Because of their huge popularity, the Cassidy Westerns extended their lengths, and it was not uncommon for them to run as long as eighty minutes. However, their scripts became overly simple, and their action content, even after Boyd had learned to ride well, remained mild. The good Cassidy Westerns of this middle period, films such as *Texas Trail* and *Bar 20 Justice,* remained

Honor of the Range (Universal, 1933), with Ken Maynard

135

Smoking Guns
(Universal, 1934),
with Ken Maynard

Smoking Guns (Universal, 1934),
with Ken Maynard, Walter Miller

West of the Pecos (RKO Radio, 1934),
with Richard Dix, Fred Kohler

The Dawn Rider (Monogram, 1935):
John Wayne, Yakima Canutt

When a Man's a Man (Fox, 1935):
George O'Brien, Dorothy Wilson,
Paul Kelly, player

Law of the 45's
(Beacon, 1935):
Al St. John,
Big Boy Williams

Red River Valley (Republic, 1935): George Cheseboro, Gene Autry, Smiley Burnette, Charles King

Toll of the Desert (Steiner, 1935): Tom London, Fred Kohler, Jr., player, Edward Cassidy, Betty Mack and (on ground) Earl Dwire

Cyclone of the Saddle (Superior, 1935): Rex Lease, Janet Chandler

Bulldog Courage (Puritan, 1935): Tim McCoy, Joan Woodbury

Border Brigands (Universal, 1935):
Buck Jones, Fred Kohler

The Way of the West (Superior, 1935):
William Desmond, Wally Wales

Cheyenne Tornado (Willis Kent, 1935): Reb Russell and production manager Bart Carre doubling as a bit player

superior products, but too many of them were bland and lacking in excitement. They all had the advantage of first-rate photography and outstandingly beautiful locations though. Even a dull film like *Cassidy of Bar 20* was consistently good to look at. In the forties, however, the Cassidys were to improve; their scripts were strengthened and their action content increased.

Warner Brothers produced only two Western series in the thirties. First there was the John Wayne series, actionful, but assembly-line jobs, and later the Dick Foran musical Westerns. Although these, like the Waynes, used a great deal of stock footage from the silent Ken Maynards, they were slicker and much more polished. Foran sang well, but in an effort to sell him to the youngsters, he tended to indulge in too much small-boy sentiment, and the dialogue in his films was often artificial, dime-novel stuff. But the ploy worked—his films *were* popular with children. Moreover, their solid production values enable them to stand up well today, with Foran himself, through no fault of his own, the only weak element in them. Foran's popularity caused him to be promoted to dramatic features, and Warners then gave up "B" Westerns entirely, although in the forties they expanded their "A" Western output, and also made two series of Western shorts.

Universal was the one major company that maintained a full "B" Western schedule without even a pause for stock-taking when talkies came in. In the early thirties, Ken Maynard and Tom Mix were their key cowboy heroes. Maynard, who in the sound era was to fluctuate between major companies and cheap independents, was no longer in his prime and did not take well to dialogue. But he had his own unit, and his films were far from formula. He wrote many of his own stories, which were often bizarre and incredible in the extreme. *Honor of the Range* had him playing a dual role as twin brothers, one weak and cowardly, the other strong and noble. *Smoking Guns* was a weird melange of spooky "old house" thrills, crocodiles in South American jungles, and enough illogical plot twists and coincidences to put Erich von Stroheim's *Queen Kelly* to shame! But, if nothing else, the Maynard Universals were colorful and unpredictable, and certainly full of action.

Tom Mix's series for Universal tried hard to duplicate the formula of his successful Fox films, going in for both rugged action and good stories, as in *Destry Rides Again,* or for an all-out circus approach, best typified by *My Pal the King.* This was a Ruritanian adventure in the *Prisoner of Zenda* manner and offered Mickey Rooney as a boy king, much stunt action, and a lively climax in a dungeon slowly filling with water. At one point Mix came "out" of the picture to address the audience directly, asking them to put themselves in the place of the little boy king seeing his first rodeo, and this simple little device worked well in rendering the rest of the exaggerated melodramatics acceptable. Mix's speech was bad, unfortunately. He slurred his words and read his lines with apparent disinterest. But he carried his years well, was still an expert rider, and managed his other action with a modicum of doubles.

To follow the Mix series, Universal signed Buck Jones. His initial group of Westerns was of exceptional quality. Films like *Border Brigands, Rock Rhodes* and *The Crimson Trail* had good scripts and top-grade action content. Later groups unfortunately suffered from budget cuts, too much talk and not enough action, although they still retained an above-average quality. And of course the Jones personality made up for many other shortcomings. While at Universal in the thirties, Jones also made four Western serials: *The Roaring West* was all action and no plot and *The Phantom Rider* was all plot and little action, but *Gordon of Ghost City* struck a happy medium, and *The Red Rider* was best of all. Its dialogue was naturalistic, its action a little more inventive than the confines of the serial usually permitted, and there were several unusual plot twists. The villain (Walter Miller) left unwitting clues to his identity by discarding his marijuana cigarettes at the scene of the crime. No critical issue was made of this vice, and it certainly in no way impaired Miller's ability to evolve inspired criminal schemes on the spur of the moment. *The Red Rider* was also notable for two elements extremely rare in the Western serial: romance and some likeable bantering comedy, the latter from the bad guys as well as the heroes.

In the late thirties, Universal attempted to change its image, and aim more at the family trade. In line with this thinking, the Karloff-Lugosi horror films were out, and Deanna Durbin was in. The rugged old Jones Westerns were replaced by an ultra-streamlined series starring singing cowboy Bob Baker. They were extremely pleasant films, with quite strong stories and beautiful locations, and their direction was often inventive. Former film editor Joseph H. Lewis (later a director of high-powered melodramas) directed many of them, and with adroit editing and camera placement, he often extracted much more punch from them than their scripts could have suggested. For they were about the most relaxed and easy-going Westerns ever made, seemingly going out of their way to avoid or minimize action. This was surprising, since Baker was a rugged fellow and an

Bar 20 Rides Again (Paramount, 1935): George Hayes, William Boyd, Paul Fix

End of the Trail (Columbia, 1936): Big Boy Williams, Louise Henry, Jack Holt

Arizona Mahoney (Paramount, 1936): June Martel, Buster Crabbe

expert rider, and occasionally could be seen doing his own stunts without a double. This series was never very popular, and at the end of the thirties Universal reverted to type with a more actionful Johnny Mack Brown series.

The only other major company to produce "B" Westerns regularly was RKO Radio, which had begun in the early thirties with a Tom Keene series. Keene was one of the more genuinely handsome Western stars, and a reasonably good if sometimes overly-enthusiastic actor. He handled his action well, although he was never wholly at ease with horses. His RKO films were carefully made and notable for big-scale climaxes, but they lacked polish, as indeed did most RKO programmers in that period. However, RKO's subsequent series with George O'Brien was a big stride forward. The O'Brien's were unusually well-made films, obviously far more expensive than the average "B" Western. They were never in the front rank of juvenile favorites, since their stress on good stories and restrained action tended to alienate youngsters, who preferred the simpler and more direct action of a Ken Maynard. But on the other hand, their very quality enabled the O'Briens to appeal to adults as well, and as a result they got far better

bookings, often at big circuit houses, than the majority of "B" Westerns. *Racketeers of the Range* and *Lawless Valley* were the best of this very distinguished series.

Undoubtedly the most prolific producer of Westerns during the thirties (or any other period) was Republic Pictures, an initially small independent company that grew out of the even smaller Mascot Pictures. Through a concentration on quality Westerns and serials, Republic amassed profits that ultimately enabled it to expand to major company status. Even when it did so, it sensibly maintained a large schedule of its bread-and-butter Western product, while adding many big-scale color Westerns as well. However, like Paramount, Republic seemed to lack the knack of transposing the speed, slickness and energy of its smaller Westerns to its bigger ones. With the exception of a brace of specials by John Ford and Raoul Walsh, most of its large-scale Westerns—even the John Wayne vehicles—tended to be slow-moving, studio-bound, and overloaded with characters and expensive décor. But Republic's "B" Westerns were perfect examples of streamlined assembly-line products. Factory products they certainly were, formularized in cast and plot. Plots at Republic were conspicuous for their lack of enterprise and substance and for the num-

Desert Gold
(Paramount, 1936):
Tom Keene,
Marsha Hunt,
Buster Crabbe

Swifty
(First Division, 1936):
Bob Kortman,
June Gale,
Hoot Gibson,
Wally Wales

ber of times they were remade with an astonishing absence of variety. One could take an early John Wayne story-line and follow its loyal service through the years as it was adapted to the needs of Roy Rogers, Bill Elliott and others, ultimately winding up with John Wayne again. Key action footage was repeated endlessly, and even songs were doctored—even by just one word—so that an "old" Roy Rogers song like "Roll On Texas Moon" would re-emerge as a "new" Rex Allen song, "Roll On Border Moon." But if one can carp at this economy-minded pillaging of content, no such complaints could be levelled at these films' most important ingredients, action and production values. From the beginning, Republic got more excitement into their chases, more pep into their stunts, and more punch into their fights, than any other studio. Camerawork was always clean, sharp and crystal clear, and locations first-class. Republic also built up an outstanding library of musical themes: *pastorale, mysterioso, agitato.* Their musical scores were among the best in the business. Few "B"

Westerns could long escape the taint of standardization, and since the key requirement of the "B" was action, it hardly mattered that Republic's machinery showed. It was exceptionally well-oiled machinery and operated flawlessly.

Republic got under way with good if straightforward series with Bob Steele, Johnny Mack Brown, and John Wayne, but first made audiences and exhibitors really sit up and take notice in 1935-36 with two new series. *The Three Mesquiteers,* based on characters by William Colt MacDonald, launched one of the most expert and enjoyable of all Western series. Even the stories (initially based on MacDonald's novels) were a decided cut above the average Republic standard. The characters were obviously harmless plagiarisms from Dumas' Three Musketeers, and they enjoyed a similar romantic and adventurous cameraderie. Ray Corrigan, Bob Livingston, and Max Terhune played the heroic trio in the early and best entries in the series, though later on John Wayne, Tom Tyler, Bob Steele, Duncan Renaldo, and

141

Rebellion (Crescent, 1936),
with Rita Hayworth, Tom Keene

Cherokee Strip (Warner Brothers, 1937),
with Edmund Cobb, Dick Foran

North of the Rio Grande (Paramount, 1937), with William Boyd

The Law West of Tombstone
(RKO Radio, 1938), with Harry Carey

Panamint's Badman (20th Century-Fox, 1938): Noah Beery Sr.,
Smith Ballew, Pat O'Brien, Stanley Fields

The Black Bandit
(Universal, 1938),
with Bob Baker,
Marjorie Reynolds

143

Pioneer Trail (Columbia, 1938):
Jack Luden, Joan Barclay

Phantom Ranger (Monogram, 1938):
Tim McCoy, Karl Hackett, Charles King

Outlaws of Sonora (Republic, 1938): Jack Ingram, Bob Livingston, Ralph Peters, and double for Livingston (playing a dual role)

Gun Packer (Monogram, 1938), with Jack Randall

Colorado Sunset
(Republic, 1939):
Smiley Burnette,
Ethan Laidlaw,
Gene Autry,
Barbara Pepper

Raymond Hatton (plus sundry unfunny comic "pals") were utilized too. In terms of period, the films were inconsistent, to say the least: the very first film was set in the immediate post-World War I years, and the heroes were veterans making a rather incongruous covered-wagon trek to the West in search of new homes. Other installments in the very long-running series were set in the Old West, in Civil War days, and, in the mid-forties, in contemporary World War II, since the West was then overrun by Axis spies seeking either mineral deposits or wild horses for use on the battlefields! But at least the Three Mesquiteer films (before the inevitable decline in their final year or two) were consistent in their fast, clean, uncomplicated action entertainment. The stunt work, usually organized and performed by Yakima Canutt, was of the highest calibre, and the chases, shot from a new camera car of which Republic was very proud and used constantly, were unusually smooth and exhilarating. *Heart of the Rockies, Range Defenders,* and *Outlaws of Sonora* were the best of this fine series, which was so successful that it naturally prompted many imitations.

But even more far-reaching was the influence of a Gene Autry Western that Republic offered in 1935, *Tumbling Tumbleweeds.* Autry was a former singer of cowboy songs on radio, and had starred in Mascot's science-fiction Western serial *Phantom Empire,* as well

as having minor roles in two Ken Maynard Westerns. *Tumbling Tumbleweeds* was a fairly straightforward Western, though on a slightly bigger scale than most, and with a large quota of songs. Although Ken Maynard, much earlier, had been the first to introduce songs into his movies, they were brought in naturally and unobtrusively, and in any case Maynard's singing voice was so unremarkable that the musical element of his films was neither stressed nor exploited. But the first Autry release was so successful that Republic immediately devised a new and unique formula for him. Songs and hillbilly comedy (largely supplied by Smiley Burnette, a fixture in all the Autry films) were given equal prominence with action, and indeed in many rural areas it was these elements that were the key box-office attractions.

The remarkable thing about the Autry Westerns is how quickly they, and Autry, improved and acquired a definite style of their own. The initial films were a trifle uncertain in what approach to take, a little disjointed in their action and the musical elements were often clumsily introduced. Autry's riding and athletic abilities were limited at first, although this was not too apparent since unusual skill was brought to bear in the use of doubles, and clever editing and camera trickery often made it look as though Autry was indeed pulling off tricky action stunts. But within two years, a bright, breezy, thoroughly entertaining formula had evolved. By now Autry had increased his riding and athletic skills ten-fold, and his originally rather colorless personality had become a most engaging one. He never aspired to the acting standards of a Buck Jones, but on the other hand his scripts seldom required him to. Warmth and geniality were enough. To offset expected criticisms that this new brand of musical Western was a travesty of tradition, Republic set them in their own never-never land, placing them quite apart from other Westerns. The earlier "historical" Cavalry-vs.-Indian Westerns that Autry had made—*Ride, Ranger, Ride* and *The Singing Vagabond*— were abandoned in favor of entirely modern Westerns. Autry frequently played a rodeo or radio star (and always under his own name); the props included high-powered cars, army tanks, airplanes, and radio stations; and the plots touched on contemporary politics, big business, social problems (the dust bowl), dairy farming as opposed to cattle ranching, problems of soil erosion and crop destruction by weeds. Against this thoroughly modern background, the traditional action ingredients— runaway stagecoaches and bar-room brawls, to say nothing of cowboys toting guns and engaging in full-scale range wars—were incongruous indeed, but here the musical elements came to the rescue. Short-skirted, glamorous cowgirls paraded down Western streets urging the populace to vote for Sheriff Autry; the villains operated lush Broadway night clubs in small Western towns where their potential customer list must have been nil; ranch owners usually had palatial homes back East, where their pretty and spoiled daughters lolled around swimming pools in brief bathing suits. All of this obviously artificial glamor and song put the Autry films into a deliberate kind of horse-operetta framework which disarmed any criticism. Admittedly, at times the song and frolic aspect dominated out of all proportion, to the extent that some of the films had almost no action at all. But on the whole the balance was well maintained. Autry's stock company of directors, cameramen, musicians and players (June Storey was a lovely and most engaging leading lady in many of his films) knew what was expected, and they delivered it. In terms of quality (if not of popularity) Autry's peak arrived in late 1937, and was maintained through 1939 with such films as *The Yodelling Kid from Pine Ridge, In Old Monterey* and *Colorado Sunset. South of the Border,* a big hit because of its popular title song and added production values, caused the Autrys to be upgraded into bigger, longer, slower (and more musical) productions temporarily, but without any lessening of Autry's popularity. In fact, he was consistently listed in the "Top Ten" money-making polls taken annually among American

Colorado Sunset (poster)

exhibitors, along with prestige stars like Clark Gable, Gary Cooper, and Deanna Durbin. While some of Autry's Westerns were relatively serious—*Sierra Sue* for example—the biggest successes were those which most fully exploited their freedom from convention, such as *South of the Border* with its improbable South American revolution and spy tale, and a heroine who enters a convent!

The fantastic public response to the Autry musical Westerns naturally produced singing cowboys from all sides. Some of them were even better singers and/or actors than Autry, but they lacked the magic combination of Autry's personality and Republic production know-how. Tex Ritter, Bob Baker, Jack Randall, Smith Ballew, James Newill, Fred Scott, and Dick Foran were among the would-be Autry successors, and still more followed in the forties: Jimmy Wakely (who copied Autry slavishly, even to using identically designed shirts and costumes), Eddie Dean, Monte Hale, and Rex Allen. Even the little-seen all-Negro Westerns (incredibly inept, and containing more self-imposed racial stereotypes than "white" Hollywood ever created) discovered their own singing cowboy in Herb Jeffries. Bearing titles like *The Bronze Buckaroo* and *Harlem Rides the Range,* they were Westerns that obstinately refused to deliver the fast action that their audiences wanted. The producers took their small units out to excellent loca-

tions, and then lacked the know-how to follow through. The sparse fights were clumsy and unconvincing, and the chases were even worse. The plots were the standard Western themes, with stock dialogue amplified and exaggerated until, unwittingly, it reached near-burlesque proportions. Interestingly enough, there was no inverted racism in these films. The stories took place in a totally black West; there were no whites in them at all, even as villains! Yet the prolonged and padded comedy relief invariably consisted of the kind of material (the comic pal scared of ghosts, the chicken-stealing cook, the crap-shooting, lazy roustabouts) which the Negroes understandably objected to in regular Hollywood films. Apart from the "personality" stars like Herb Jeffries, the acting level was low, although the casts remained fairly constant from film to film, with the same comics and heavies. While the veteran Sam Newfield directed one or two of them, most of these Westerns were made by inexperienced Negro directors. The musical element was not stressed, and Jeffries was really the only singing cowboy that this small group produced.

But the most successful of them all, and the only one ever to challenge Autry's supremacy, was Roy Rogers, who had played singing and other bits in several Autry and Mesquiteer Westerns and who was developed by Republic in 1938 as a second-string Autry. At first his films had very much a pattern of their own: they re-

Desperate Trails
(Universal, 1939).
A new team:
Bob Baker,
Johnny Mack Brown,
Fuzzy Knight

Desperate Trails (Universal, 1939)

Crashing Thru (Monogram, 1939): Roy Barcroft, Milburn Stone, James Newill

A Monogram Tex Ritter unit on location at Kanab, Utah: director Spencer Bennet (with hat) seated by camera, producer Edward Finney (hatless) on truck at extreme right

Arizona Legion (RKO Radio, 1939): George O'Brien, Laraine Johnson (Day), Edward Le Saint

Roll Wagons Roll (Monogram, 1939), with Tex Ritter

mained traditional historical and action Westerns, with songs introduced casually, if frequently. Rogers had a likeable personality but was of slim build, and didn't seem a very formidable opponent for the imposing array of villains that the studio lined up for him: Fred Kohler, Cyrus Kendall, Noble Johnson. Nevertheless, the early Rogers Westerns had flair and style. In the early forties, however, they began to emulate the Autry films more openly, although with such a down-playing of action content and often such a total avoidance of fisticuffs that juvenile support and enthusiasm was slow in coming. However, when Autry joined the armed forces during World War II, Republic got behind the Rogers films with a big "King of the Cowboys" campaign, and built Rogers into a major star. His films, many of them remakes of earlier Autry successes, were given far bigger budgets than had ever been allocated to Autry, and for a time the formula was almost destroyed through imbalance. An over-stress on music—not just songs but mildly spectacular production numbers and long fiesta and nightclub sequences—often crowded the action ingredients out almost entirely, and such Westerns as *Idaho* and *The Cowboy and the Senorita* could far more logically have been labelled merely musicals. The costumes employed by Rogers, heroine Dale Evans, and the singing group The Sons of the Pioneers became more reminiscent of uniforms or Broadway chorus line costumes than of authentic Western regalia, and only comedy relief Gabby Hayes was left as a link with the Westerns of old. However, with Rogers firmly estab-

Shooting a riding closeup from a camera car

lished, the always economy-conscious Republic saw no need to continue with these musical spectaculars indefinitely, and gradually the budgets were lowered and the musical elements reduced. Towards the end of his contract at Republic, when his films were being made in Trucolor, there was even a drastic shift of emphasis so that music almost disappeared, and action was *over-*emphasized via often extremely savage and bloody fight scenes, and unpleasant plot-lines in which murders, beatings, and the mistreatment of animals became unnecessarily prominent.

While the Rogers Westerns never quite duplicated the freshness of the Autrys, at their best (in the 1942-43 years, when Rogers was being built up but hadn't yet been thrust into the inflated musicals) they had a sober and realistic quality and a neat blending of song and action. *Heart of the Golden West, Silver Spurs,* and *The Man From Music Mountain* are especially notable Rogers Westerns from this period.

Monogram (which had a longer history than Republic, with roots in the old Rayart company of the twenties) in a sense paralleled Republic through the thirties, but never equalled it. Their first sound West-

erns, with Bill Cody, Bob Steele, Tom Tyler, and Rex Bell, were indistinguishable from most other independent Westerns of the period, though their plots were sometimes a cut above the average. Tom Tyler's *Partners of the Trail* was unique in having no villains, an element of mysticism, a hero accused of the murder of his wife, and a strong prison-cell scene of the hero going beserk, that was shot *almost* in the style of German expressionism. Monogram drew its Western stars from the ranks of those who had slipped slightly or newcomers on the way up. After John Wayne left Warners, he made a series for Monogram of extremely uneven quality. Some, like *The Trail Beyond,* were marathons of action, others were dull and pedestrian. If nothing else, they were unique in their stunt action. Yakima Canutt was their perennial villain *and* double for Wayne; as a double he was frequently photographed in semi-closeup, and in the climactic sequences he could often be seen literally chasing himself. Also during the thirties Monogram turned out enjoyable series with Tom Keene, Tim McCoy, Tex Ritter (whose films were often built around stock footage going as far back as Thomas Ince's *The Deserter!*), and Jack Randall. Monogram had one of

The on-screen image: *Renegade Trail* (Paramount, 1939), with William Boyd

larger production, and may well have come to John Ford's attention, for its similarities to his *Stagecoach* of the following year are unmistakeable. Monogram was to improve the overall quality of its "B" Westerns in the early forties, and later on would make isolated "A" Westerns superior to the average Republic product, but the studio was to remain permanently in Republic's shadow.

A youthful Roy Rogers, riding Trigger; biggest new Western star of the late thirties.

the best Western ranch locations of any studio, located in Newhall, and in Harry Neumann they had an excellent cameraman too. Their basic weakness was in allocating bigger than usual budgets to the first films in any given series, establishing a level of quality, and then cutting the budgets drastically so that that quality was not maintained. A good example were the Jack Randall Westerns, initially produced by Scott R. Dunlap, and given excellent production mountings, only to slip back to a routine level after a handful of first-class films. Randall's first film for Monogram, *Riders of the Dawn,* has real class and a brilliantly staged, photographed, and stunted climax. It is a running gun battle between a posse of lawmen and the villains, some of whom are in a stagecoach. The effectiveness of the climax was increased by its utilization of the Hopalong Cassidy formula—a fairly slow and methodical build-up to this prolonged climax, and the sudden introduction of background music to underline its action. This final chase, staged on salt flats, would have done credit to a much

10

THE THIRTIES

The spectacular upsurge in both the quantity and quality of the "B" Western throughout the thirties was hardly matched by a corresponding increase in the big-scale Western. Most of the major companies hardly bothered with the "A" Western. Fox, even though it had John Ford under contract for the entire period, didn't offer him a single horse opera, and indeed avoided the genre almost entirely. *Ramona,* the old Indian romantic tragedy, was remade primarily because it afforded an excuse for using the newly-perfected three-color Technicolor. A medium-budget Cisco Kid adventure with Warner Baxter was a long way below the standard of Raoul Walsh's original, but did serve to pave the way for a later continuing series, with Cesar Romero. MGM made an occasional Wallace Beery good-badman Western, à la *The Badman of Brimstone,* and also used the Western format to turn Robert Taylor and Nelson Eddy into "he-men" when their glamorous, romantic roles began to fade in popularity. Two of the Nelson Eddy-Jeanette MacDonald operettas, *Rose Marie* and *The Girl of the Golden West,* might also be termed fringe Westerns. William Wellman's *Robin Hood of Eldorado,* a romanticized but rugged biography of the bandit Juaquin Murietta, was the best of MGM's handful of Westerns.

The Columbia schedule was totally devoid of major Westerns, although some of their programmers had a quality which indicated that they might well have benefitted from more ambitious treatment. *The End of the Trail,* from a Zane Grey story, was unique in both its plot (starting with the Spanish-American War, it followed its protagonists through to modern racketeering in the contemporary West) and in its use of an "anti-hero" long before either the expression or the type became commonplace. It must also rank as the only Western in which the hero (Jack Holt) went to the gallows at the end for killing the villain—an unusually poignant and well-played scene that must have wreaked havoc on unprepared juvenile audiences.

Universal's sole spectacular of the thirties was *Sutter's Gold,* a project originally designed for the great Russian director S. M. Eisenstein, who ultimately never worked in Hollywood at all. Drastically reshaped as a vehicle for Edward Arnold it was also intended to re-establish director James Cruze and be a talkie equivalent of *The Covered Wagon.* Unfortunately, it was. Despite a crowded canvas it was a jerky, episodic tale, frequently held together by old-fashioned subtitles, and with its action sequences staged on a big scale but disappointingly underplayed. Its length, its lack of big star names, and its much higher than anticipated budget all but wrecked Universal, which would have been crippled by this one film had not a real blockbuster, *Show Boat,* come along to bail them out at just the right time.

Until 1939, Warner Brothers, too, kept away from the big Westerns, catering to the action market with their Errol Flynn swashbucklers, their crime films, and their rugged Technicolor Northwoods adventures—*God's Country and the Woman, Heart of the North, Valley of the Giants.*

Actually, by far the best Warner Western of the thirties was *Massacre* (1933), a film which really grew out of their series of social protest melodramas. Richard Barthelmess played a successful rodeo Indian star who returns to his reservation, only to find his people cheated by their white overseers and dying of disease and starvation. A little known film even in its day, and never revived, *Massacre* was probably the best talkie of director Alan Crosland, who had been at the peak of his prestige in the late twenties with such films as *Don Juan* and *The Jazz Singer.* The story is perhaps more than a little influenced in its structure by *I Am a Fugitive from a Chain Gang,* and like most of the other social essays of the early thirties, its framework is a melodramatic one in which the scales of social comment are decidedly loaded—it does seem unlikely that *all* of the white Indian Affairs officers were corrupt thieves, rapists, lechers and drug addicts! But since the story hardly claims documentary status and since like Zane Grey's *The Vanishing American,* the story is a darned good one, the out-

Secrets (United Artists, 1933), directed by Frank Borzage, with Mary Pickford, Leslie Howard

155

The Plainsman (Paramount, 1936), directed by Cecil B. DeMille with Gary Cooper and Jean Arthur as a glossy Wild Bill Hickok and Calamity Jane

Three Godfathers (MGM, 1936), directed by Richard Boleslawsky, with Chester Morris

Robin Hood of Eldorado (MGM, 1936), directed by William Wellman; Warner Baxter, Bruce Cabot, Margo

Sutter's Gold (Universal, 1936), directed by James Cruze, with Edward Arnold

The Texas Rangers (Paramount, 1936), directed by King Vidor; Hank Bell, Jack Oakie, Edward Ellis, Fred MacMurray

It Happened in Hollywood (Columbia, 1937), with Richard Dix, Billy Burrud, Fay Wray

Rose Marie (MGM, 1936), with Jeanette MacDonald and Nelson Eddy

spoken and obviously sincere social overtones come as something of a bonus. It offered fine camerawork with striking images and well-chosen locations, powerfully done mob scenes, and much casual race humor (a Negro valet constantly makes cracks about Indians, whom he considers *his* social inferiors).

RKO Radio maintained a fairly regular output of medium budget Westerns, stronger on plot and casts than on action: *Powdersmoke Range,* in which they gathered together such an all-star cast of current and former Western stars that there was almost no time left for story or action; *The Arizonian,* a good Richard Dix vehicle; and, best of all, *The Last Outlaw,* a strong John Ford story (unfortunately not directed by him) about an old-time outlaw returning from jail to the modern West to find himself up against prejudice, modern rack-eteers, and—a neat touch—townsfolk who were entranced by the new singing cowboy Westerns in their theatre! Harry Carey played the old-timer, and a particularly good cast backed him up: Hoot Gibson, Tom Tyler, Henry B. Walthall, and current singing cowboy star Fred Scott.

The only remaining major company, Paramount, had

Wells Fargo (Paramount, 1937), directed by Frank Lloyd; with Frances Dee, Joel McCrea

Way Out West (Hal Roach-MGM, 1937), with Laurel & Hardy

158

no difficulty in effectively monopolizing the epic Western in the thirties. There was no competition. Unfortunately Paramount, always so expert in less ambitious Westerns, never mastered the knack of turning out big-scale ones equally well. (Exceptions to this are some of their post-1950 Westerns directed for them by John Ford and others; but by then the system of studio control and contract players and directors had undergone great changes, and the later Ford and Howard Hawks Westerns were thus merely financed and released by Paramount, not physically produced by them.) By far the best of Paramount's quartet of mid-thirties epics was *The Texas Rangers,* and indeed, despite its weaknesses, it is still one of the most enjoyable Paramount super-Westerns from any period. It was directed by King Vidor in 1936, his first Western since *Billy the Kid,* and a much more polished if less gripping work. While his Civil War film of the year before, *So Red the Rose,* suffered from too many good authors trying to change perfectly good hokum into something worthy of literary respect, the script of *The Texas Rangers* was not ambitious enough. Vidor wrote it himself, ostensibly basing it on Texas Rangers records, but actually it seems to

The Texans (Paramount, 1938),
with Randolph Scott, Joan Bennett

Frontier Marshall
(20th Century-Fox, 1939),
with Randolph Scott,

159

Union Pacific
(Paramount, 1939),
directed by Cecil B. DeMille,
with Joel McCrea,
Barbara Stanwyck

The Girl of the Golden West (MGM, 1938), with Jeanette MacDonald and Nelson Eddy

consist of a couple of well-known Ranger incidents (referred to in brochures issued by the now very publicity-conscious Ranger headquarters in Amarillo) fused with a very standard "B" picture plot which constantly threatens to reduce its epic stature.

The often trite and artificial level of dialogue doesn't help either. But Vidor fills his film with enough incident, action, and well-developed characters for these flaws not to matter too much. (Just how good the film is one can tell from a look at the dull Technicolor forties remake, *Streets of Laredo*. The Indians were deleted from that version entirely, along with all the epic qualities, and overdoses of sex and brutality were added. The basic illustration in all of the ads was of a sadistic flogging, an element not present in the original film at all.) *The Texas Rangers* is full of pleasingly heroic images and has a stirring musical score borrowed partially from *Old Ironsides*. The staging of the action is splendid (the Indian fighting scenes originally involved use of the enlarged Magnascope screen), the horse falls and stunts lively, and the editing sharp, although, curiously, as in *The Covered Wagon*, there is no intercutting of the Cavalry riding to the rescue in the Indian battle sequences. Vidor was too good a director not to know the value of cross-cutting, but in this instance he probably

160

Union Pacific

felt it would have been too much of a "B" picture cliché to use. The locations are impressive and unfamiliar; most of the film was shot out of doors, making the occasional studio "exteriors" (Indians rolling rocks over a cliff) stick out like sore thumbs, but these scenes are few and largely for matching-up or cutaway purposes. Even though not a classic, *The Texas Rangers* is an exhilarating Western with a refreshing schoolboy vigor. It also was fortunate in having one of those key scenes that made a vivid impression and is constantly talked about as one of the cinematic highspots of the thirties—Lloyd Nolan's callous murder of his friend Jack Oakie, shooting him in the belly from under a table while smiling and talking in tones of friendship and devotion.

Paramount's other big super-Western of 1936, and to the studio a much more important property, was Cecil B. DeMille's *The Plainsman,* with Gary Cooper as Wild Bill Hickok. Although DeMille had flirted with Western themes earlier, this was his first full-scale epic, and while it was a big popular success, it was hardly a good picture. Its script was heavy-handed and obvious, and far too much of the film was spoiled by DeMille's over-fondness for shooting as much of his pictures as possible within the confines of the studio. He was a director whose sense of efficiency demanded that every

studio facility, every piece of equipment, every department head, be on call at all times. He was a showman like Ziegfeld rather than an artist like Griffith, and he only functioned well on his home studio ground. (Big action sequences that had to be shot outside the studio were usually handled by second unit directors like Arthur Rosson, their skill and exciting staging minimized when they were later intercut with prolonged studio-filmed inserts.) At a time when Harry Sherman was producing the "B" Hopalong Cassidy Westerns for the same studio and using superb locations with nary a process screen in sight, it was jarring indeed to find DeMille in *The Plainsman,* with its huge budget, intercutting genuine exteriors with the most patently phony studio duplicates, bobbing his actors across the screen on mock-up horses, and using back projection techniques throughout.

Nevertheless, despite the omnipresence of the process screen and a few big silent stock shots, the production as a whole was big and certainly entertaining. Jean Arthur, playing Calamity Jane for glamor and blonde hair (a far cry from the homely, wizened woman that was the real Calamity Jane!) was even less realistic than Doris Day, who later played Jane in a Technicolor musical. But audiences of the thirties were not inclined

Stand Up and Fight (MGM, 1939), directed by W. S. Van Dyke, with Robert Taylor, Wallace Beery

Destry Rides Again
(Universal, 1939),
directed by George Marshall,
Marlene Dietrich,
Una Merkel

to carp at seeing a current top favorite in such a perfect showcase role. And DeMille never missed a chance to drop a historical name or two, or ram home a sledge hammer point. The film opened with Abraham Lincoln being dragged away from an all-important meeting at which the destiny of the West was about to be settled because a nagging Mrs. Lincoln, warned him that he would be late for the theatre!

Slowly paced, but colorful, filled with interesting characters and well-knit, *The Plainsman* may be all corn and contrivance, but its machinery works well, and it is easy to see from it why DeMille had such a hold on audiences for almost a half-century. More show than film, it is also a major landmark in the movie treatment of Wild Bill Hickok, who, from William S. Hart and

Gary Cooper, gradually lessened in box-office stature (Richard Dix, Bruce Cabot, Roy Rogers, Ted Adams, Douglas Kennedy, Tom Brown) and heroic status until, in the fifties (with films like *I Killed Wild Bill Hickok*) he underwent a strange moral metamorphosis to become accepted, without buildup or explanation, as a villain. Attempts by Western historians, largely during the forties, to destroy the myth and show that Hickok was human and not a god, first set him up as merely a bully and a showoff, then as a lecher and a coward, and finally as an outright killer. The ultimate was probably reached in 1953's *Jack McCall, Desperado* in which McCall (a virile, upright George Montgomery, as opposed to cowardly, sneaking Porter Hall in DeMille's film) justifiably shoots murderer and thief Hickok in a

Stagecoach (United Artists, 1939): Yakima Canutt taking a horse fall

164

fair fight, and is acquitted by the court. (Conveniently, that film forgot to mention that McCall was retried by a different court and promptly hanged.)

For all their script weaknesses, *The Texas Rangers* and *The Plainsman* were both deserved popular successes, but Paramount was unable to duplicate that success in its follow-ups. *Wells Fargo* (1937) was a long, carefully made, but stiff, dull and practically actionless movie, long on historical data, romance, and interior scenes, short on excitement and exteriors. Like all Frank Lloyd epics, it was treated in tableau form, with the characters rather lifelessly symbolizing progressive pioneering, self-centered greed, and so forth. The method had worked superbly well for Lloyd's ver-

sion of Noël Coward's *Cavalcade,* but it never worked on his several epics of American history. Later reissues edited the film drastically, but such editing could only shorten it, not accelerate its leaden pace. The following year's *The Texans,* another remake of *North of '36,* was hardly more successful, though a trifle more animated. Despite a good cast (Randolph Scott, Joan Bennett, May Robson) and a good story of a cattle drive in post-Civil War days, it looked like what it was: an attempt to make an "instant" epic with the snappier pace of Paramount's smaller Zane Grey Westerns and with a great deal of borrowing of stock footage. It was big, but disjointed, clumsily put together, and lacking in any kind of style.

Man of Conquest (Republic, 1939): Canutt again at the Battle of San Jacinto

Fortunately for Paramount, however, the success of *The Plainsman* had spurred DeMille into producing another Western spectacle as an immediate follow-up, and in 1939 he released one of his best pictures, *Union Pacific*. Although it covered the same historical ground as John Ford's *The Iron Horse* (and even copied one or two sequences rather too carefully), it had a better script and one in which personal relationships and motivations were appropriately subordinated to the basic theme of empire building. Furthermore, DeMille kept his action—a couple of fights, a train hold-up, an attack by Indians, a train wreck in a snowy pass, the destruction of the villain's saloon, the climactic street shootout—fairly constant and regularly spaced, instead of compressing all of his action into single highlight sequences as he had done in *The Plainsman* and would do again in his dullest and slowest Western, *North West Mounted Police*. The overdone Irish blarney of Barbara Stanwyck apart, the acting from a first-rate cast was uniformly good, and there was a far more satisfying level of intelligent and non-obtrusive comedy than one usually found with DeMille. *Union Pacific* was one of 1939's blockbusters, and in those days such major films were slower in getting into general release than is the practice today. By the time it had played out its advance "prestige" dates and had gone into general release, the outbreak of World War II was that much nearer. Few people in the United States believed that this country could actually be embroiled in a war, but feeling ran high against Nazi Germany, no one could deny that there were dark days ahead, and patriotic zeal that had lain dormant for almost two decades was suddenly rekindled. Unwittingly, *Union Pacific* catered to that zeal, and its climactic moments, promising blood and toil, with some kind of Utopia "at the end of tracks," were both prophetic and topical. A good film by any standards, *Union Pacific* undoubtedly had its box-office potential boosted by a wave of national feeling with which it coincided in so timely a fashion.

However, *Union Pacific* was too much of an isolated film, too atypical of the Western genre, to bring the Western back to life on its own. That minor miracle was wrought by a far less ambitious film, John Ford's *Stagecoach*, which preceded it in release by a month or two. A superb film, *Stagecoach* caught the imagination of both critics and public. It was both entertainment and poetry, and it made an instant star of John Wayne. More to the point, it was directly responsible for the biggest single cycle of large-scale Westerns that the movies had ever known: Westerns of every variety, Westerns in Technicolor, Westerns with bigger-name stars than had hitherto condescended to appear in them.

Ruth Roland, queen of silent Western serials

The boom continued for a full three years, even upgrading the quality of "B" Westerns, too. While the freshness began to fade in 1942, the popularity of the Western had been too firmly re-established and entrenched for it ever to disappear from the screen again. The history of the Western since 1942 has not been one of diminishing and subsequent re-vitalizing; it has instead been one of constant popularity, the changing cycles representing only the waves of changing tastes: the Western with Sex; the Western with Brutality; the Western with Psychology. Even the Westerns that spoofed themselves—and a cycle of self-burlesque is usually a sign that a genre has played itself out—were followed by yet more cycles (including the unexpected popularity of the German and Italian-made Westerns) which merely confirmed that while the Western had nothing intrinsically new to say, it was constantly finding new ways to say it.

166

In the silent era, the quantity of Western serials produced ran second only to the mystery and detection serial, a genre that, despite its need of exposition and lengthy dialogue titles, proved to be well suited to the silent film. In sound films however, the Western moved easily into first place. In a way, and notwithstanding the enormous popularity of the Western, this was surprising. For one thing, by its very nature a matter of familiar formula, the Western was limited in its kind of action: dynamited shacks, lynch mobs, stampeding herds of cattle or buffalo, falls from cliffs or into mine shafts, burning at the stake by redskins, an occasional flood or avalanche, falling under an Iron Horse or once in a while an ore-crushing machine—that about summed up the spectrum of perils that could be presented. Not only is the list so limited that the average fifteen-chapter serial found itself repeating situations within its span, but of course these same situations were spilling over into other serials *and* the regular feature Westerns. Yet despite a format which permitted less deviation and variety than the science fiction or adventure serial, the Western serial always flourished—even overcoming the problem of thin plot material which too often, even with the legitimately episodic theme of a wagon train trek—became little more than a series of casually related fights and chases. Occasionally though, the serial allowed itself the luxury of stepping outside the already strained bounds of logic of the traditional Western, and mixed science-fiction, Nazi spies and sundry other melodramatic detours into the hopper.

Republic undoubtedly made the best Western serials, just as it made the best "B" Westerns, but Universal (in the early thirties) and Columbia (in the early forties) produced some good ones too. Most of the big Western stars—Buck Jones, Ken Maynard, Tim McCoy, William Desmond, Art Acord, Bill Elliott, Johnny Mack Brown, Tom Mix, and even Gene Autry—made serials at one time or another in their careers.

The Perils of Pauline (Eclectic, 1914), with Pearl White and Crane Wilbur

167

Hawk of the Hills (Pathé, 1927),
with Walter Miller,
Chief Yowlachie, Allene Ray

Whispering Smith Rides (Universal, 1927), with Wallace MacDonald

Last of the Mohicans (Mascot, 1932): Hobart Bosworth is held prisoner at left, while Bob Kortman threatens Harry Carey

The Miracle Rider (Mascot, 1935): Tom Mix (his last film) versus Tom London

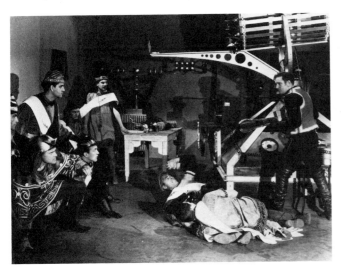

Phantom Empire (Mascot, 1935): Gene Autry about to turn a ray gun on the citizens of Murania

The Vigilantes Are Coming (Republic, 1936): Robert Warwick and Fred Kohler, representing the Red Menace in old California, temporarily have the advantage of Bob Livingston

The Painted Stallion (Republic, 1937): Ray Corrigan and Jean Carmen

The Painted Stallion: Jack Perrin, Hoot Gibson, Ray Corrigan, Sammy McKim, Hal Taliaferro

Wild West Days (Universal, 1937): Walter Miller, erstwhile silent serial hero, was Universal's stock villain in the thirties; with Alan Bridge

The Lone Ranger (Republic, 1938): Lane Chandler, Lee Powell, Bruce Bennett, George Montgomery and Hal Taliaferro, with Chief Thundercloud as Tonto

Custer's Last Stand (Louis Weiss, 1936): Typical of the stiffly posed publicity stills that often contained more action than the film itself. Bobby Nelson is apparently blowing the bugle to warn the battling trooper in the foreground that he's about to be shot in the neck by his own corporal.

Overland Mail (Universal, 1942): Lon Chaney battles Charlie Stevens (a grandson of Apache warrior Geronimo)

170

King of the Mounties (Republic, 1942): During the war, the Axis powers found tremendous military and espionage potential in the West! William von Brincken, Nestor Paiva and Abner

Biberman plot diabolical strategy that is backed up by such secret weapons as this flying wing.

Winners of the West (Universal, 1940), with Dick Foran somewhere under that wagon

11

THE FORTIES - A PEAK OF POPULARITY

Without for one instant belittling the importance of *Stagecoach* as a film, not a little of its success with the critics can be ascribed to its snob value. It was based on a novel by Ernest Haycox, itself regarded as a minor classic of the genre, and both novel and film had their original roots in de Maupassant's "Boule de Suif." So it was on firmer literary ground than any talkie Western since *Cimarron,* and de Maupassant, even if only remotely connected with it, still carried more prestige than Edna Ferber!

With the exception of the big Indian chase, it either avoided such traditional Western action as the fist-fight, or, as in the climactic shoot-out in the streets, staged most of it off-screen and suggested more than it showed.

For all of its Fordian sentiment and a rich gallery of fairly standardized types, it was a new kind of Western, literate, visually poetic, and thus one that could be praised without the lowering of one's own standards. It was the first time that Ford had used Utah's Monument Valley as a location, and the breathtaking scenic grandeur of the film impressed the critics too. But to a man they seemed to miss the beauty of the writing, camera-work, and art direction in the sequence near the end wherein the hero walks the prostitute-heroine through the streets of Lordsburg, from the bustling Main Street to the shadowy and raucous red light district which is to be her new home. Although the film is slow in getting under way, the gallery of colorful portraits (Carradine,

Berton Churchill, and Donald Meek in particular) sustained interest until the magnificently staged highlight of the chase across the salt flats. (Magnificent, but unrealistic; it was pointed out somewhat caustically by Bill Hart that the Indians, being the intelligent warriors that they were, would have shot the horses first and ended the chase before it began!) But with its vivid action, dynamic horse falls, and other stunt work engineered by Yakima Canutt, and heroic images in the finale—the cavalry bursting on to the screen in a sustained running insert, all waving banners, bugles and swords outstretched for the charge, nobody felt inclined to criticize Ford for this deliberate oversight. Obviously *Stagecoach* was not the screen's first adult Western, its first poetic Western, or its first literary Western, but it was the first one in a long while to combine those elements so effectively. Its enormous popularity was understandable; equally so the prolific new cycle of deluxe-scale Westerns it prompted. What was surprising was that none of its immediate offspring even attempted to duplicate its artistic standards, but were content to be big "shows." They covered every dramatic and historic aspect of the Western spectrum, but in terms of big-scale action, as showcases for the now more prevalent Technicolor, or as vehicles for stars (Errol Flynn, Robert Taylor, Jon Hall, Franchot Tone, Tyrone Power, Henry Fonda, Ray

Stagecoach (United Artists, 1939), directed by John Ford

Milland, James Cagney) not normally associated with the Western.

Wayne and Claire Trevor were immediately re-teamed in two big historical Westerns. *The Dark Command* (directed by Raoul Walsh), based on W. R. Burnette's book about guerilla leader Cantrell, had a good deal of merit, but was marred by typical Republic shortcomings, such as Gabby Hayes comedy injected in an effort to keep the "hick" audiences happy. However, it was a carefully made film, the best of all the deluxe Republic Westerns. The second Wayne-Trevor vehicle, *Allegheny Uprising,* was a rather plodding film for RKO dealing with the Revolutionary War. So malapropos did it seem at the time to remind the British (then engaged in fighting a war with America as a non-combatant ally) that they had once fought against America, that it was never released in Britain.

Despite the great number and variety of Westerns being turned out in late 1939 through 1942, they all seemed to fall into one of three categories. First and foremost there were the historical Westerns; secondly, there were the whitewashed biographies of outlaws, and in terms of sheer quantity this category rapidly moved into first position; and thirdly there were the comedies and the spoofs. *Destry Rides Again* worked a peculiar

kind of chemistry in its teaming of Marlene Dietrich and James Stewart. It was actually a dull and uneventful Western, weak on both story and drama, full of cliché; yet the dynamic Dietrich personality plus a memorable musical score and a cast full of enjoyable character players somehow held it all together and turned it into a freak box-office smash. Despite its tragic ending—a hackneyed situation dating back to *Under Two Flags* and beyond—it was basically a kind of tongue-in-cheek *The Blue Angel,* and not unreasonably has been credited with introducing sex to the Western. Today its sex content seems innocuous in the extreme, yet it was the first big step along a new road for the Western. Over the next very few years, others would take it several steps farther: the sensationalism of Howard Hughes' *The Outlaw,* the piquant sex-farce of that much underrated comedy Western *Frontier Gal,* the hard-breathing passion of King Vidor's *Duel in the Sun.* But for the time being it seemed that *Destry Rides Again,* in the forefront of this new Western boom, at the same time made it possible for the Western to kid itself.

Western satire has never been markedly successful, either aesthetically or commercially. The best were the Sennett and Fairbanks spoofs of pre-1920. Too many of the later "satires" merely put stand-up comedians in

North West Mounted Police (Paramount, 1940), directed by Cecil B. DeMille with Gary Cooper, Madeleine Carroll, Robert Preston, Paulette Goddard, Preston Foster, Lynne Overman

174

Stagecoach: Joe Rickson, Tom Tyler and Vester Pegg as the Plummer Boys

Geronimo (Paramount, 1939): Preston Foster, William Henry and extras shooting at back-projected stock-shot Indians from *The Plainsman*

Dodge City (Warner Brothers, 1939), directed by Michael Curtiz, with Errol Flynn

Arizona (Columbia, 1940), with William Holden, Jean Arthur, directed by Wesley Ruggles

Santa Fe Trail (Warner Brothers, 1940), directed by Michael Curtiz with Raymond Massey as John Brown

The Dark Command (Republic, 1940), directed by Raoul Walsh with John Wayne; Quantrell's raiders

The Dark Command: Claire Trevor, Roy Rogers, Walter Pidgeon

Western Union (20th Century-Fox, 1941), directed by Fritz Lang

Western surroundings and allowed them to play out their normal routines on horseback. Jack Benny's *Buck Benny Rides Again* fell into that category, as did most of Abbott and Costello's *Ride 'Em Cowboy.* But the Marx Brothers' *Go West* did have moments of genuine and very funny satire and a wild train ride climax that was as thrilling as it was imaginative in its sight gags. Allan Dwan's *Trail of the Vigilantes,* clearly trying to recapture the spirit of *Destry Rides Again* and using many of the same character players, was a most enjoyable romp, but it never became true satire. Perhaps because of the skill of the action scenes, and the suave, straight playing of villain Warren William, it seemed to divide itself into two distinct halves. Most of the comedy was placed in the first half, while the second half with all the action, whether intended or not, emerged as good, straight Western fare.

Warner Brothers, whose only genuine epic Western in the thirties had been the off-beat but sluggish *Gold Is Where You Find It,* suddenly embraced the genre wholeheartedly with one of the most enjoyable of all good badman movies, *The Oklahoma Kid,* and the first of the big Errol Flynn outdoor epics, *Dodge City.* Prototype of all the honest-lawman-cleans-up-Sin-Town Westerns of the early forties, *Dodge City* was bland, simple in its distinctions between good and evil, and full of big-scale, sprawling action, with an all-out stunt saloon battle a special highlight. It was filmed in superlative Technicolor and needed it; later reissues in black and white showed how much gloss and production value the film had gained just from its color. It seemed to lose scope and size in plain black and white. Its follow-ups, however, were shot in black and white, and the money thus saved was put to better use with good scripting and solid production values. *Virginia City,* which co-starred Flynn with Randolph Scott and utilized Humphrey Bogart as a sneering but none too convincing Mexican bandit, was slow in getting itself started but more than made up for this in its second half. Even better was *Santa Fe Trail,* a more compact, better-written Western dealing with John Brown's Kansas rebellion prior to the Civil War. Flynn again starred, Raymond Massey was Brown, and the climax was a well-staged reconstruction of the battle at Harper's Ferry.

For sheer size, Warners surpassed themselves with their next and most expensive Flynn epic, *They Died With Their Boots On,* the story of General Custer. Although it directly contradicted *Santa Fe Trail* in several key historical details, it was a colorful cavalcade, one of the very few Westerns to deal cohesively with the Civil War, its aftermath, and the gradually increasing warfare between whites and Indians. Long, studded with name

They Died With Their Boots On (Warner Brothers, 1941), directed by Raoul Walsh, with Errol Flynn

players, full of lavish sets, with Custer's Civil War glories and his ultimate massacre at the Little Big Horn as genuinely spectacular action highlights, it was nevertheless a rather stiff and ponderous film for all of its care and generous budget. It was the last of the Warner spectaculars for a long time, their Westerns soon becoming standardized products, and by the end of the forties, often mere programmers of seventy minutes or less, vehicles for the now slipping Errol Flynn and Dennis Morgan. Throughout the rest of the forties, their best Westerns fell into groups other than historical epics, although Flynn's *San Antonio* did produce a temporary revival of the old flair, with a beautifully staged (if overwrought) mass gun battle as its climax.

The epics from other companies were variable. Columbia's *Arizona* brought Wesley Ruggles back to the genre for the first time since *Cimarron*. Its attention to detail was commendable, the reconstruction of old Tucson realistically done, and some of the scenes of mass movement—the Union troops' evacuation of Tucson, for example—superbly organized. But it was a slow and tedious work, the footage devoted to the personal stories of its somewhat uninteresting principals swamping what *should* have been the dominant theme, the development of the territory of Arizona. *Texas,* which followed, likewise played down its epic potential, but at least was lively, fast, and full of rather refreshingly grisly black humor. Columbia was to make more

The Great Man's Lady (Paramount, 1941), directed by William Wellman, with Joel McCrea, Barbara Stanwyck

Texas (Columbia, 1941), directed by George Marshall; George Bancroft, William Holden, Glenn Ford, Raymond Hatton

Honky Tonk (MGM, 1941), directed by Jack Conway; Clark Gable, Chill Wills, Lana Turner, Frank Morgan

Water for Canitoga (1942): A German reconstruction of a frontier town

and more super-Westerns as the forties progressed, but they were all as standardized as its "Bs." MGM's only genuine epic of the forties was King Vidor's *North West Passage,* hardly a Western in the traditional sense, though interesting in its refusal to gloss over the horrors of any kind of warfare and in removing the Seventh Cavalry brand of glamor from its grim Indian fighting scenes. MGM (as did RKO) produced a number of "pocket" epics with James Craig, films like *Gentle Annie,* all surprisingly weak and uninteresting works. Fox's huge success with *Jesse James* brought them back to the western fold with a vengeance, but with a concentration on outlaw "biographies." Fox's best traditional epic was Fritz Lang's *Western Union,* in which the historically uneventful construction of the telegraph system was spiced up with Indian raids, outlaw intervention, and a big forest fire. As in most Lang films, the villainy was made far more interesting than the dull heroics. *Brigham Young* was a reasonably reliable account of the Mormons' wagon trek to Salt Lake, its opening sequences of religious persecution far more dramatic and powerful than the later pilgrimage footage, which contained fine panoramic vistas of wagon train and prairie but little else. William Wellman's "biography" of Bill Cody, *Buffalo Bill,* included a well-done battle in a river between cavalrymen and Indians, but otherwise was slow and historically suspect. Fox, too, tended to let its Westerns slide after the early forties, and, aside from John Ford's superlative *My Darling Clementine* drift into the formula pattern of *Fury at Furnace Creek.*

With one notable exception, Paramount spent time, money, big stars and good directors on its initial epics of the forties, though with results even less satisfactory than those achieved in the thirties. But the film that fired the opening salvo in their cycle was the particularly inept *Geronimo* of late 1939, rushed into production to cash in on the Indian warrior who had acquired a new fame via *Stagecoach. Geronimo* was a fascinating example of literally a million dollars' worth of production value being squandered on a mere programmer. Every foot of major action material was lifted bodily from *The Plainsman, The Texas Rangers, Wells Fargo* and even silents. The plot itself, complete even to much of the dialogue, was a reworking of the 1933 *Lives of a Bengal Lancer.* Nobody had the nerve to claim a story credit for the mélange, so it was allocated to the director, Paul Sloane, who probably deserved it for his cunning in maneuvering around the old footage. The cast, made up primarily of lesser Paramount contractees, was notable mainly for being one of the few non-"B" films to give Chief Thundercloud any kind of a role (he

played *Geronimo*) and for affording Gene Lockhart yet another opportunity for cringing and whining as only he knew how. Leading lady Ellen Drew, second in the long cast, had what was surely one of the most non-taxing roles in movie history. Given a word or two of dialogue at the beginning of the film, she was promptly involved in a stagecoach wreck lifted from *Wells Fargo,* and spent the rest of the movie in bed and in a coma.

Paramount's more ambitious new epics were less stingy with their budgets, but even less productive of excitement. DeMille's *North West Mounted Police* was a top-heavy, star-laden Technicolor vehicle that meandered along endlessly, and *California,* a Ray Milland-Barbara Stanwyck opus, was a dull, unofficial remake of *The Covered Wagon. Rangers of Fortune* tried, futilely, to repeat the formula of *Three Godfathers,* and putting Paramount's hottest male star, Alan Ladd, into the West didn't help either. Despite a good story and cast, his *Whispering Smith* was still a bore, lacking all the expertise that Paramount had been able to bring to its "B" products. The new version of *The Virginian,* with Joel McCrea effectively cast in the old Gary Cooper role, was also a slow and tame production. It had always been a deliberately slow-paced tale, but at least the 1929 version had had a certain integrity, and a real sense of time, place, and people. The new one had pleasant Technicolor exteriors and nothing else. Eventually Paramount turned over much of its Western schedule to quickie producers Bill Pine and Bill Thomas. Their Westerns (*El Paso, Albuquerque,* and others) were no great shakes either, but at least they were unpretentious and delivered enough routine action to make them commercially profitable.

Not a major success at the time, but one of the most durable of the new Western cycle was Sam Goldwyn's *The Westerner* of 1940. Although directed without any marked personal style by William Wyler, it provided Gary Cooper with one of his best roles and was a sober, naturalistic, beautifully photographed film. Action was handled in a restrained, often almost deliberately awkward style, never becoming a slick stuntman's circus. However, it was Walter Brennan's role as the famous—or notorious—Judge Roy Bean that dominated the film and much later became the basis of a television series.

Two of the most enjoyable epics came not from the major studios at all, but from the independents. Republic's *Man of Conquest* is still the best movie biography of Sam Houston and, John Wayne's grandiose budget for *The Alamo* notwithstanding, the best account of Texas' fight for independence against the forces of Mexico's Santa Ana. A shade too measured in its detailing of Houston's two marriages and his relationship

Duel in the Sun: Otto Kruger, Joseph Cotten, Hal Taliaferro, Harry Carey

Red River (United Artists, 1948), directed by Howard Hawks, with John Wayne, Montgomery Clift

Duel in the Sun (Selznick, 1946), directed by King Vidor, with Gregory Peck Jennifer Jones

The Oklahoma Kid (Warner Brothers, 1939), directed by Lloyd Bacon; Lola Lane, James Cagney

with Andrew Jackson, it nevertheless made the development and birth of a great state understandable as no other similar movie had. Moreover, it made the most of its limited resources, and created by sheer excitement that which it could not afford to do by size. Its climactic Battle of San Jacinto, staged by stunt maestros Reeves Eason and Yakima Canutt, was relatively brief and small-scale, yet far more vigorous than the long-sustained battle scenes in *The Alamo*. Richard Dix, of course, was a perfect choice for Houston.

Edward Small's *Kit Carson* was a second pleasingly unpretentious epic of the period, although for director George B. Seitz it was another flawed work. His silent *The Vanishing American* for Paramount had had an important theme, stunning photography of Monument Valley locations, a fascinating documentary prologue detailing the history of the Indian, a dramatic opening stressing the role of the Indian in World War I, and his right to full citizenship privileges—and then the film took a cheapjack descent into melodrama. *Kit Carson* had many advantages—a good cast, fine locations, a solid enough script with some above-average writing, in spite of some unnecessary romantic and comic intrusions. Unfortunately, the budget seemed to exhaust itself just when it was needed most, and the film fizzes out lamely at the end, its final battle a mess of evasions, economies, studio sets, and back projection. But at least Seitz had had his big Indian battle, which occurred at the midway point. Beautifully shot and staged, it was the best "traditional" Indian fight—hordes of warriors surrounding a ring of covered wagons—since *The Big Trail*.

But it was a concentration on the badman and a concerted attempt to whitewash such legendary outlaws as Jesse James and the Daltons that really dominated the big-scale Westerns of the early forties. Appropriately, it was *Jesse James* in 1939 that gave this branch of the Western its biggest boost. Although Jesse undoubtedly was victimized by the railroads and their land-grabbing agents, as were many other Missouri farmers, Nunnally Johnson's screenplay nevertheless rather overdid the circumstances that forced him into outlawry. In Tyrone Power's hands, Jesse was all warmth and nobility, with none of the meanness and killer instinct that apparently characterized the real Jesse. But regardless of its distortions, to say nothing of its reshaping what must have been a remarkable and dramatic life into standard Hollywood scenario form, this *Jesse James* carried a lot of incidental truth along with it. Henry King was a director singularly at home with the American scene, whether history or rural romance. He had gone spectacularly awry when tackling biblical spectacle or exotic adventure, but with his feet firmly planted in American soil

Jesse James (20th Century-Fox, 1939), directed by Henry King, with Tyrone Power, Henry Fonda; bank holdup sequence

and folklore, he has given us such interesting films as *Tol'able David, The Winning of Barbara Worth* and *The Gunfighter.* Much of the background milieu of *Jesse James* seems exactly right, and Henry Fonda's performance as Frank James (a role he repeated in a sequel directed by Fritz Lang) is quiet and effective, stealing the thunder from Power not only because he was a better actor, but because the role itself was more thoughtfully conceived. Purely on the level of the Western, *Jesse James* was too plodding, too generous in its footage to that shameless old barnstormer Henry Hull, and surprisingly lacking in a true sense of tragedy for its climax, something that King brought off rather better in *The Gunfighter.* But the Technicolor photography was exceptionally fine, there was a first-rate use of authentic outdoor locations with an absolute minimum of studio "exteriors," the two big chase scenes were excitingly done, and there were some outstanding stunt scenes with horses—a charge through a store window, falls in a bank robbery sequence, and leaps from high cliffs.

The Oklahoma Kid, which went into release almost simultaneously, was generally far more to the liking of the Western traditionalists. Here was a big-scale Western that never once allowed its size to create an aura of self-importance. It moved from start to finish, maintained a pleasant tongue-in-cheek approach (which made the occasional starkly tragic moments stand out in even greater relief), and was so much in the spirit of the silents that it even resorted frequently to titles to bridge transitions. Cagney brought his cheeky big-city personality to the West without making the slightest change in his standard characterization, and Bogart, black-clad, twitching, as the wholly evil Whip McCord, played it completely straight, without even the mordant sense of humor that he brought to his gangster roles. Even with two such big names on hand, the climax was the time-honored fistic set-to in the local saloon. James Wong Howe's photography gave the film visual class throughout, and even if unimportant as a film, *The Oklahoma Kid* is notable as one of the very few "A" Westerns that was able to duplicate the speed and zip of the "B."

The stream of outlaw movies that followed these two far outnumbered the historical epics that grew out of *Stagecoach.* MGM produced a Technicolor *Billy the Kid* with Robert Taylor that, except for a well-done climactic chase, was a weak and totally re-written "adaptation" of the same book by Walter Noble Burns that had formed the basis of King Vidor's film a decade earlier. The renewed popularity of the Western also allowed MGM to expand and increase its "good bad-

When the Daltons Rode (Universal, 1940), directed by George Marshall, with Randolph Scott, Kay Francis; excellent stuntwork in a train holdup sequence

Billy the Kid (MGM, 1941), directed by David Miller, with Robert Taylor, Brian Donlevy

man" vehicles for Wallace Beery, and to afford them far better production values than their rather hackneyed scripts deserved. *Wyoming* opened with a good train hold-up and closed with a well-done Indian attack, but in between limped along with far too many sentimental exchanges between Beery and Bobs Watson. (Watson was a moon-faced youngster whose specialty was instant and non-stop blubbering; *Dodge City* earned the eternal gratitude of sorely-tried moviegoers of the forties by allowing him one such crying marathon and then having him killed off by Bruce Cabot's outlaws!) *Wyoming* was filmed almost entirely on location against majestic mountain ranges and wide expanses of prairie, captured in crystal-clear and well-composed images by Clyde de Vinna, who had photographed the early McCoy Westerns. But dramatically it was inferior to its visuals, although at least the Beery personality was colorful. Later in the forties, when Beery's larcenous heart was softened by the wide eyes of Margaret O'Brien, the overdoses of sentiment became too much, although their *Bad Bascomb* did partially redeem itself in an excellent climax.

Fox whitewashed bandit queen Belle Starr (in the person of Gene Tierney) even more than Jesse James, and Universal performed a like operation on the Dal-

Belle Starr (20th Century-Fox, 1941)

Badmen of Missouri (Warner Brothers, 1941), directed by Ray Enright, with Arthur Kennedy, Dennis Morgan and Wayne Morris as the Younger Brothers

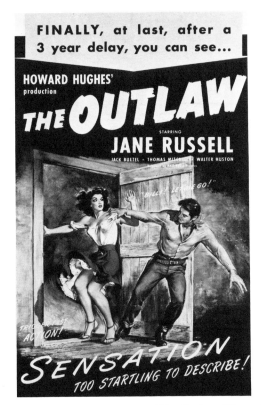

The Outlaw (Howard Hughes, 1943), directed by Hughes and
Howard Hawks

Black Bart (Universal, 1948),
with Dan Duryea

Rangers of Fortune (Paramount, 1940), directed by Sam Wood, with Patricia Morrison, Albert Dekker, Gilbert Roland, Fred MacMurray

Trail of the Vigilantes (Universal, 1940), directed by Allan Dwan, with Franchot Tone

Twenty Mule Team (MGM, 1940), with Wallace Beery, Leo Carrillo

tons. However, *When the Daltons Rode* was one of the best of the outlaw cycle, well-directed by George Marshall, and with some breathlessly exciting hold-up and chase sequences. Its script tended to follow formula lines, and its historical veracity was suspect, since it had the Daltons being wiped out to a man in its climactic raid on the Coffeyville bank—even though the film's scenario was based on a book by a surviving Dalton! Warners added a biography of the Younger Brothers to the prevailing outlawry, and the "name" outlaws were soon depleted. However, the genre remained a popular one, and there were always lesser miscreants like Sam Bass and the Sundance Kid to be unearthed. Just as the horror film, to boost flagging box-office interest, was teaming up the Frankenstein Monster, Dracula, and the Wolf Man, so did the Western take to teaming up the James Boys, the Daltons, the Youngers, Belle Starr, and others in medium-budgeters like *Badmen's Territory*. RKO made something of a specialty of these, with Randolph Scott the overworked marshal striving to maintain law and order in the face of such all-star banditry.

By 1942, the concentration on deluxe-scale Westerns levelled off, and in their place came a steady flow of Westerns that rated "A" playing time because of their length and star casts, but were relatively unambitious in theme. Some of these proved to be among the most enjoyable Westerns of the forties. Universal's *The Spoilers,* with its unbeatable star combination of John Wayne, Randolph Scott, and Marlene Dietrich, and with such reliables as Richard Barthelmess, Harry Carey, and William Farnum in support, is still the best of that (thus far) five-times-filmed actioner, with its grand-scale climactic fight a minor masterpiece of stunt action, skillful doubling and tight editing, if a lesser masterpiece of realism. Any one of the blows struck in that fight would have felled an ox, so the staying power of Scott and Wayne through a whole reel of such manhandling was a little hard to take. RKO, too, turned out some exceptionally good Westerns in this period, notably Robert Wise's *Blood on the Moon* (still one of his best films and one of the best scripted Westerns of the forties) and *Tall in the Saddle,* a good John Wayne vehicle.

In a budgetary sense, a new kind of "B" Western was evolving in these years. Universal was making "in-between" Westerns of the calibre of *Badlands of Dakota, Men of Texas* and *Frontier Badmen*—historical Westerns of minor epic stature that contained few real highlights but moved constantly and made maximum use of studio contract players. Their slightly increased budgets and added lengths enabled them to play as top features in less important situations and as co-features on the big

Texas Rangers Ride Again (Paramount, 1940), with John Howard, Ellen Drew

The Westerner (United Artists, 1940), directed by William Wyler with Gary Cooper, Doris Davenport

Go West (MGM, 1940), with the Marx Brothers, Diana Lewis, John Carroll

Wild Bill Hickok Rides (Warner Brothers, 1941), with Bruce Cabot, Warren William

The Westerner: Walter Brennan as Judge Roy Bean

Men of Texas (Universal, 1942): Robert Stack, Leo Carrillo, Jackie Cooper, Frank Hagney

Salome, Where She Danced (Universal, 1945): Rod Cameron, Walter Slezak

In Old Oklahoma (Republic, 1943), with John Wayne

Frontier Gal (Universal, 1945), with Rod Cameron and Yvonne de Carlo

The Kansan (Harry Sherman-United Artists, 1943): Robert Armstrong, Richard Dix, Clem Bevans

Along Came Jones (International-RKO, 1945), with Gary Cooper and Loretta Young

186

Canyon Passage (Universal, 1946), directed by Jacques Tourneur; Ward Bond, Dana Andrews

Abilene Town (United Artists, 1946): Jack Lambert, Randolph Scott

The Ox-Bow Incident: scene illustrative of stress on studio "exteriors" in the forties

The Plainsman and the Lady (Republic, 1946):
Bill Elliott, Andy Clyde, Donald Barry, Joseph
Schildkraut, Charles Judels

The Angel and the Badman (Republic, 1947), with
John Wayne and Gail Russell

Blood on the Moon (RKO Radio, 1948), directed by
Robert Wise; with Robert Mitchum, Barbara Bel
Geddes

Yellow Sky (20th Century-Fox, 1948), directed by
William Wellman, with Gregory Peck, Anne Baxter

circuits. They were a highly profitable group. Harry
Sherman, producer of the Hopalong Cassidy Westerns,
also produced a series of these films cleanly photographed, well cast, a little slowly-paced but with big-
scale action climaxes to compensate. Richard Dix starred
in the majority of the Sherman films, and one of the
best, *Buckskin Frontier,* was a model of how to make
a pocket *Iron Horse* and make it look far more expensive than it was.

Sherman's success with these films tended to make
some of the later ones too pretentious for their own
good. *A Woman of the Town* tried for dramatic and
emotional impact at the expense of action and was a
little too precious in its name-dropping. A young lady
reporter in Bat Masterson's office is told to stick to her
gossip column, and a "throwaway" line as subtle as a
sledge hammer identifies her as Louella Parsons! But
on the whole Sherman's standards were high, and at
least two of his more ambitious films, *Ramrod* (directed
by André de Toth) and *Four Faces West* (directed by
Alfred E. Green), both starring Joel McCrea, were
unusually appealing, dramatically strong, intelligently
written, and if not major artistic or box-office land-

marks, then certainly among the most satisfying Westerns of the period.

As the forties progressed, the films in the budgetary
classification of *Badlands of Dakota* gradually needed
an extra ingredient to sustain their box-office value, and
so color was added. Universal and Columbia in particular increased their output of medium-budget eighty-
minute color Westerns with such stars as Randolph
Scott, Rod Cameron and George Montgomery. Universal evolved a particularly pleasing format for these
films, and some, like Joel McCrea's *Saddle Tramp* were
exceptionally good. Begun before television became
serious commercial competition to the movies, these
expensive-looking Westerns were actually fairly economical to make and also proved useful proving grounds
for the various new color systems of the forties—Cinecolor, Trucolor, Anscocolor. However, while the overall
quality and widespread production proved to be an
effective answer to the cheaper Western fare seen on
television in that medium's earliest days, their very
quality helped hasten the demise of the standard six-
reel "B" Western.

At the beginning of the forties, the "B" Western, too,

The Untamed Breed (Columbia, 1948), with Sonny Tufts

Rough Shod (RKO Radio, 1949), directed by Mark Robson; with Robert Sterling and Gloria Grahame

Stampede (Allied Artists, 1949), directed by Lesley Selander; with Rod Cameron

Three Godfathers (MGM, 1949), directed by John Ford, with Harry Carey, Jr., John Wayne, Pedro Armendariz

Streets of Laredo (Paramount, 1949), with MacDonald Carey, William Bendix, William Holden

benefitted from the resurgence of interest in the species. It was still possible to make "B"s economically and with style. Republic was at its peak, not only producing the Gene Autry, Roy Rogers and Three Mesquiteers series, but also introducing new stars (Sunset Carson, Allan Lane, Red Barry) as well as utilizing well-established ones (Bob Livingston, Bill Elliott). Republic's Westerns were still essentially formula pictures, more action than plot, but within that formula they were expertly done and made by some of the very best directors in the field: Lesley Selander, William Witney, John English. And since Republic still had John Wayne for a series of big-scale Westerns (*In Old Oklahoma, Dakota, The Angel and the Badman*), it remained very much the leader in the Western field. Monogram, however, was improving the quality of its product considerably, most notably in the excellent "Rough Riders" series co-starring Buck Jones, Tim McCoy and Raymond Hatton. Produced by the veteran Scott R. Dunlap, whose Westerns always had that little extra polish and care that makes all the difference, the Rough Riders films placed more emphasis on characterization than on action, but they were unusually smoothly made, and at first at least, willing to spend additional money for such added touches as worthwhile locations, first-rate utilization of camera trucks for running inserts, and the creation of new musical scores. Jones, McCoy, and Hatton made one of the best co-starring trios of any Western series, and the first three entries, *Arizona Bound, The Gunman from Bodie,* and *Forbidden Trails,* were quite outstanding. Thereafter, the usual Monogram policy of slashing budgets and eliminating location work took its inevitable toll, and later films in the series were disappointingly substandard, although the work of the three stars remained enthusiastic and interesting. Jones' tragic death in the Cocoanut Grove fire brought the series to an end after its first season.

However, its success had spurred a number of imitations, most notably Monogram's own *Trail Blazers* series with Ken Maynard, Hoot Gibson, and Bob Steele. These films were lamentably lacking in the finesse of the Dunlap predecessors; their production values were crude, their scores, by Frank Sanucci, repetitious and (to be charitable) unmelodic, and their stories merely pegs on which to hang action. But they *were* fast and deliberately designed to exploit spectacular stunt-work. Although the publicity claimed that these veteran stars were still scorning doubles, the use of Cliff Lyons and other stuntmen in the action scenes was often painfully apparent. Maynard was by now rather clumsy, and his delivery of dialogue even more awkward, but Gibson had maintained a relatively slim build, a naturalistic

Best co-starring trio of the forties: Buck Jones, Tim McCoy and Raymond Hatton as the Rough Riders (Monogram)

Another Three Mesquiteers grouping: Raymond Hatton, Duncan Renaldo, Bob Livingston (Republic)

More Mesquiteers: Rufe Davis, Tom Tyler, Bob Steele (Republic)

Imitation Mesquiteers: Max Terhune, Ray Corrigan (both of the original Mesquiteer series) and Dennis Moore as The Range Busters (Monogram)

A "Range Busters" variation: John King, David Sharpe, Max Terhune (Monogram)

Gene Autry (Republic)

Dale Evans, George "Gabby" Hayes and Roy Rogers (Republic)

acting style, and his old sense of humor. Both he and Maynard still managed to do a goodly portion of their own riding. (Use of doubles in Westerns is, in any case, not entirely a matter of ability. Expediency enters into it, too, since a second unit can be shooting long shot action scenes with doubles while the main unit shoots the closeup and dialogue footage).

Monogram's "Cisco Kid" series started off rather weakly with Duncan Renaldo, shifted profitably to Gilbert Roland, and under the sponsorship of producer Scott Dunlap, added production values and better scripts. The Roland Cisco Kids had genuine charm, a quality rarely found in "B" Westerns, and their polish more than made up for their comparative dearth of action. *Beauty and the Bandit* was possibly the best of this most enjoyable series.

Jimmy Wakely, in a pedestrian musical Western series, and Whip Wilson, in a so-so series, also appeared on the Monogram schedules in the forties, but its longest-running series was a Johnny Mack Brown group designed to replace the Rough Riders. Some sixty-six of them were made. Small-scale, often sparse in action content, they were nevertheless pleasing little films. Raymond Hatton co-starred in the majority of them, and the early ones clearly inherited several unused Rough Riders scripts. Again, when producer Dunlap stepped in to make a personal production or a special, the quality rose to a marked degree. *The Gentleman from Texas,* produced by Dunlap and directed by veteran Lambert Hillyer, was quite the best of this series.

RKO continued to make the most expensive and polished "B"s. George O'Brien was still turning out exceptionally good Westerns in the early forties, and a Tim Holt series, also of good quality, was started too. A brief Zane Grey series offered Robert Mitchum in two and then James Warren in several. These were soon terminated, but the Holt series continued until the fifties.

Ownership of several Zane Grey properties also prompted Fox to begin a fresh series of program Westerns in the forties. The first, *Riders of the Purple Sage,* was that rare animal, a remake superior to at least some of its predecessors. In less than an hour, it packed in all of Grey's complicated plot, managed to prevent the unusually large number of characters from getting in each other's way, offered plenty of action and good locations and photography. It was a "class" film all the way, lacking only the finesse of background music. George Montgomery starred, and was promptly put into a follow-up, *The Last of the Duanes.* However, Montgomery, like Mitchum at RKO Radio, was almost immediately elevated to big picture stardom. A new "discovery," John Kimbrough, took over at Fox. His

Buck Jones with veteran producer-director Scott R. Dunlap, who was responsible for the "quality" Westerns at Monogram

Allan Lane (Republic)

Sunset Carson (Republic)

Anne Jeffreys, Bill Elliott, and Gabby Hayes (Republic)

Gilbert Roland (Monogram)

Monte Hale (Republic)

Johnny Mack Brown and Nell O'Day, hard-riding duo of Universal Westerns

Tom Keene and stunt-rider Evelyn Finley (Monogram)

Russell Hayden and William Boyd (Paramount)

Don "Red" Barry (Republic)

Hoot Gibson and Ken Maynard (Monogram)

Tex Ritter and his producer Edward Finney, with Suzan Dale (Monogram)

Johnny Mack Brown and Raymond Hatton (Monogram)

Two more veterans of the silents: William Desmond and Noah Beery, Sr. (Universal)

two Westerns, *Sundown Jim* and *The Lone Star Ranger* were vastly inferior to Montgomery's, and he himself was little more than a disaster. The series was dropped.

Columbia continued to grind out slick but strictly formula Westerns, in the early forties doubling up their stars so that Charles Starrett and Russell Hayden co-starred in one group, Bill Elliott and Tex Ritter in another. Action fans had no complaints. There were often five or six fights per picture and as many chases, but not surprisingly there was little time for plot. Also, there was a hurried, cheap look to their pictures. One could always tell which company made a Western by the sound effects, and Columbia's effects for gun-shots, fisticuffs, and galloping hooves had a cheap, unrealistic sound to them, indicative of amplification or an encho chamber. Throughout the forties, the quality of Columbia's Westerns gradually declined, until Gene Autry, forming his own production outfit, came to work for the studio. Autry's first films for Columbia were vastly different from his Republic format; the plots were more sober, the musical elements restrained, the action more elaborate. Not surprisingly, the first two, *The Last Roundup* and *Loaded Pistols,* were excellent and among the best "B" Westerns made anywhere, although their extra length and budgets almost belied the "B" category. In time Autry was forced to curtail his budgets and the films became more standardized, but he did maintain good quality to the end. Columbia's final cheap Charles Starrett entries seemed doubly poor in comparison with the Autrys.

PRC (Producers Releasing Corporation), a new company set up along the lines of Monogram, but making a cheaper product, came into being in the forties too. It attracted a large number of surprisingly good Western stars such as Tim McCoy, Buster Crabbe, Bob Livingston, and Bob Steele, and some lesser ones: George Houston, Tex Ritter, James Newill, Dave O'Brien, Bill Boyd (a radio singer, not the Hopalong Cassidy star), Lash LaRue, and Eddie Dean. While some of the first McCoy and Crabbe Westerns were quite good, the studio's output as a whole was shoddy, their Westerns fast but totally lacking in any kind of polish. The exploitation of Cinecolor gave some of their Eddie Deans a superficial edge over the others, but Dean was not popular and his films eventually reverted to black and white. A New York *Daily News* critic was not impressed by one of his later works and was moved to remark: "Eddie Dean's latest is in black and white rather than color, but the improvement is hardly noticeable; you can still see him."

Universal, like Republic, was concerned more with a fast action format than with plot, an attitude rather at

Kirby Grant (Universal and Monogram)

Blazing Six-Shooters (Columbia, 1940), with Iris Meredith, Charles Starrett, Dick Curtis

Bullet Code (RKO Radio, 1940), with George O'Brien, Virginia Vale

The Golden Trail (Monogram, 1940), with Tex Ritter

Old-timer William Farnum, still kept busy at Universal

odds with its former approach to the Buck Jones and Ken Maynard films. Its Johnny Mack Brown series (initially co-starring Bob Baker, then presenting Brown solo, and concluding with a group in which he starred with Tex Ritter) evolved an ultra-streamlined approach in which directors like Ray Taylor, Ford Beebe, and Lewis D. Collins slammed over the fights and chases with tremendous gusto. Universal built up an excellent library of chase and *agitato* music, and made a fine art of the running insert. Nell O'Day, who appeared in many of the Brown Westerns, was a fine stunt rider, a big asset to the series, and a pleasant change from the usual passive heroine. Although excellent entertainment for dyed-in-the-wool fans, the sameness of this series was pointed up when a really imaginative director was put to work on one of them. Joseph L. Lewis, who directed *Arizona Cyclone,* was a former film editor, and it showed. He broke down a simple confrontation between hero and villain into a number of tense shots, cross-cut between hands poised over holsters, changed focus within the shots, and added speed and depth to his chase scenes by placing objects (trees, fences) between his camera truck and the riders, or by having his truck on a different ground level from the horses. *Arizona Cyclone* was a perfect example of how to add real style and directorial finesse without radically changing the script. But it is unlikely that his efforts brought in a nickel more than the prosaic and workmanlike methods of Lewis D. Collins. Johnny Mack Brown's likeable personality, pleasant acting style, and genuine athletic ability were also major assets of the series. He used far fewer doubles than most stars in his fights and leaps. Universal's final groups of "B" Westerns, with Rod Cameron, Eddie Dew, and Kirby Grant, were much inferior to the Browns.

By the end of the forties, the "B" Western scenes had changed considerably. Independent Westerns had all but disappeared. Many of the former top-line stars were either dead or in retirement. The quantity of "B" Westerns had been seriously curtailed. Groups of eight had been cut to groups of six, many series discontinued entirely, and thanks to the ever-rising costs of production, it was impossible to maintain the former level of quality. The Hopalong Cassidy Westerns that Harry Sherman had made for United Artists in the early forties were polished, actionful, well peopled with extras and respectable character actors, shot in good locations and in good Western street and ranch sets, were now being produced by William Boyd himself, with slim plots, meagre action, a dearth of people and livestock, and the skimpiest of sets. Even the "look" of the "B" Western had changed: the glossy, sunlit photography that had characterized the Republics less than ten years earlier had been replaced by drab, often ill-lit camerawork, shot regardless of overcast skies and apparently photographed (or processed) on much coarser film stock. It was definitely the beginning of the end for the "B" Western.

Meanwhile, the "A" Western was proliferating, and becoming increasingly thoughtful. William Wellman's *The Ox Bow Incident* was a powerful and uncompromising indictment of lynch law, marred somewhat by the forties method of shooting so much within the studio (although this did give it the controlled lighting that such a theme needed) and by a script that sometimes amplified the suggestion and understatement of the original novel unnecessarily. The post-war cycle of psychological melodramas, although primarily exploited by the big-city crime film, invaded the West tentatively but interestingly in such films as John Sturges', *Captured* and Raoul Walsh's *Pursued,* the latter a film that emulated Hitchcock's *Spellbound* in incorporating nightmarish dream sequences into its story of chase and vengeance. Another Walsh film, *Colorado Territory,* an excellent and underrated Western, was a remake of and a close parallel to his earlier Bogart gangster film, *High Sierra,* its tragic ending dovetailing neatly into the fashionable defeatism that marked so many psychological melodramas of the late forties.

1946 saw John Ford for the first time since his silent days at Universal and Fox returning to the Western on a regular basis. *My Darling Clementine,* made some seven years after *Stagecoach,* was easily one of Ford's best Westerns, its simplicity and beauty weakened only by an untypical and excessive number of closeups of Linda Darnell. (Ford was never fond of big head closeups, especially of his leading ladies, and usually eliminated them even when the scripts called for them.) *My Darling Clementine* is quite certainly the best of all the Wyatt Earp films. Without minimizing the need for "artistic freedom" or suggesting that the fiery Ford ever really kowtowed to the front office, it is a matter of obvious record that his best single group of pictures was that made for 20th Century-Fox between 1939 and 1946, a group bounded by *Young Mr. Lincoln* at one end and *My Darling Clementine* at the other (both of them Henry Fonda films, incidentally) with *How Green Was My Valley, The Grapes of Wrath,* and others in between. The common denominator of all of these films is discipline. The all look and sound like John Ford films; his favorite people and musical themes are ever-present, and whether they were photographed by Joe MacDonald or Arthur Miller they all have the same visual flow that marks a Ford picture. But somehow all

In Old Cheyenne (Republic, 1941), with Roy Rogers

Riders of the Purple Sage (20th Century-Fox, 1941): Richard Lane, Leroy Mason, George Montgomery

The Old Chisholm Trail (Universal, 1942): Roy Barcroft, Johnny Mack Brown

The Gay Cavalier (Monogram, 1945), with Gilbert Roland

Peggy Moran: typical of the vivacious and decidedly glamorous heroines who were by now invading the Westerns regularly

Flaming Bullets (PRC, 1945), with Tex Ritter and Dave O'Brien

Guest stars Allan Lane, Bob Livingston, Red Barry, Bill Elliott and Sunset Carson help Roy Rogers round up villains Roy Barcroft and Grant Withers in *Bells of Rosarita* (Republic, 1945)

The Caravan Trail (PRC, 1946), Jack O'Shea, Lash LaRue, Charles King, Eddie Dean, Emmet Lynn

Wanderer of the Wasteland (RKO Radio, 1945), with James Warren and Audrey Long

South of the Chisholm Trail (Columbia, 1946), with Charles Starrett as the Durango Kid, doubled by Jock Mahoney

King of the Bandits (Monogram, 1947), with Gilbert Roland

Indian Agent (RKO Radio, 1948), with Tim Holt and Noah Beery, Jr.

of his virtues are concentrated and utilized to the full, his weaknesses—an unrestrained sentimentality, a penchant for rowdy comedy—either diluted or kept severely in check. With *My Darling Clementine* Ford was back to the Western permanently; he would make three more in the forties, more still in the fifties and sixties.

The notoriety of Howard Hughes' *The Outlaw* (a slow film, often an inept one, but by no means as bad a Western as it is generally reputed to be) gained a further foothold for sex in the West, and King Vidor's *Duel in the Sun* was a natural successor. Forcibly expanded by producer Selznick into another would-be *Gone With the Wind,* it was literally too big and imbalanced a film for its own good. The genuinely epic qualities of the tale were reduced to background details against which the personal and largely sexual adventures of the three protagonists were played out. Nevertheless, its mass action scenes (particularly a gathering of the ranchers, to be confronted by a railroad gang and a troop of cavalry) were beautifully organized and shot, its sexual scenes had both a raw power and an erotic flavor entirely missing from *The Outlaw,* and its use of color was dynamic and daring. Intimate scenes such as the death of Lillian Gish and the impending execution of Herbert Marshall showed Vidor at his best. And Jennifer Jones was never better photographed, and never exuded more sheer animal sexuality than as Pearl. A sweeping box-office success, *Duel in the Sun* was reviewed scornfully and sarcastically, and not taken seriously. For that matter, even Ford's *My Darling Clementine* was received very coolly.

Lawless Code (Monogram, 1949): Jimmy Wakely and Terry Frost

Riders of the Dusk (Monogram, 1949): Whip Wilson and Marshall Reed

199

As far as the critics were concerned, there were only two major Westerns with artistic integrity in the forties: Ford's *Stagecoach* (even though technically a 1939 film) and Howard Hawks' *Red River* in 1948. United Artists, distributors of the latter film, built its whole ad campaign around its (presumed) reception as a classic. "In 30 years, only three—*The Covered Wagon*—*Stagecoach*—and *Red River*" was the pitch used in advertising. Although a big critical and commercial success, the film was (comparatively speaking) forgotten rather quickly perhaps because, on the surface at least, it seemed to have nothing fresh to say and to be merely an expert retravelling of old and familiar trails. The sudden cult interest in director Hawks some fifteen years later caused *Red River* to be re-acclaimed, re-appraised, and certainly over-analyzed. Hawks' films *are* complex in their character interrelationships and even in the thematic relationship of one film to another, but such an intellectual approach to *Red River* seems especially unjustified when one considers that it was conceived as a variation on and an unofficial remake of *Mutiny on the Bounty*. It has long been an old dodge to remake non-Westerns as horse operas (*Gunga Din* into *Sergeants Three, The Sea Wolf* into *Barricade*) and *Red River* is an especially adroit re-working of the earlier film, with the same conflict between the two men, the same floggings, the same mutiny—and cattle substituting for breadfruit trees. Hawks has never seemed quite enough of a sentimentalist to be as at home with the Western as he was with the gangster film *(Scarface)* or the crackling satire *(His Girl Friday)*. He deliberately plays down physical action, keeping it secondary to human conflicts, and his Westerns, *Red River* in particular, are far more in the anti-romanticist tradition of *The Covered Wagon* than in that of the warm, affectionate idylls of John Ford. And of course, no criticism is implied in this, there is certainly room for both traditions.

In 1948, however, because it was the "milestone" Western of the decade, *Red River*, far from writing "finis" to the Western, did nevertheless seem to imply that the Western had little more to say. Yet how wrong such an assumption would be. Less than two years away were two Westerns, *Broken Arrow* and *The Gunfighter*, which would not only set new standards of maturity, honesty and compassion but would launch new cycles along hitherto untravelled tangents. And waiting in the wings were the technological innovations of the wide-screen and three-dimensional processes to mirror changing content in a changing screen shape.

THE FIFTIES – AND RADICAL CHANGES

The year 1950 started the new decade off with a bang. The gradual decline and disappearance of the beloved "B" Western seemed hardly to matter in the face of three of the finest "A" Westerns Hollywood had ever produced: John Ford's *The Wagonmaster,* Henry King's *The Gunfighter,* and Delmer Daves' *Broken Arrow.* While the Indian had certainly been treated sympathetically in several films of the forties, and most especially in John Ford's beautiful, sentimental (but rather uneventful) *She Wore a Yellow Ribbon,* no film had been really unreservedly pro-Indian. *Broken Arrow,* while it may have been prompted by the controversial but commercially successful race problem (Jewish and Negro) films of the forties, managed the rare movie trick of making a social comment without overloading the scales. The side issues of *Broken Arrow* were rapidly commercialized to the hilt: it established Cochise (little exploited in such earlier Westerns as *Valley of the Sun*) as a "regular" horse opera hero, prompted sequels, established a pattern by which big male stars (Burt Lancaster, Robert Taylor, Rock Hudson, ultimately even Elvis Presley) could profitably play Indians, ushered in a whole new era of villainous whites (including General Custer!) and misunderstood Noble Redmen, and finally prompted a long-running TV series, with all the attendant merchandising of bows and arrows and Indian outfits for the kiddies. Its controlled documentary qualities were also copied shamelessly by many

202   *The Gunfighter* (20th Century-Fox, 1950), directed by Henry
King; Anthony Ross, Gregory Peck

lesser Westerns. But the original film was good enough to survive even this subsequent exploitation; it was and is a warm, poignant, often poetic film. Delmer Daves has always been an interesting and underrated writer-director, and there is little doubt that *Broken Arrow* is his best film. Even James Stewart's mannered playing is held reasonably in check. Pictorially it is often stunning, and the gentle beauty of some of the courtship scenes, and especially the simplicity of composition of the wedding night scene—white horse, brown tepee, blue skies and a scene that has the good sense to fade before it can be fully absorbed—are some of the loveliest images any Western has ever given us. If one cavils at all, it is at the compromise ending. Racial barriers being what they were in 1950, an "important" white star still couldn't be allowed to marry an Indian girl and live happily ever after. One of them had to meet an untimely end which could be twisted to symbolic purpose, and it invariably proved to be the hapless Indian girl, as witness also William Wellman's deeply felt but badly mutilated *Across the Wide Missouri*. In 1957, a much lesser Western, Samuel Fuller's *Run of the Arrow*, did allow such a union to survive. Had censorship been advanced by a few years, or *Broken Arrow* delayed for those same number of years, it might well have been the best, most honest and definitive movie on the Indian problem. As it is, it is merely the best.

Many of the Westerns of this type were directed by veterans like George Sherman, graduates of "B" horse operas, and men who really knew how to keep their films on the move. One major new name to come to the fore in this period was that of Bud Boetticher, director of some of the best Audie Murphy films, but who established his most notable relationship with Randolph Scott in a series of Westerns for Columbia and Warner Brothers: *The Tall T, Seven Men from Now,* and others. Without sacrificing any of the traditional action elements, there was somehow an extra dimension to the Boetticher Westerns; they had a biting, underplayed quality, the kind of films one would have expected had John Huston (in his prime) suddenly decided to become a director of Westerns. The French critics picked up Boetticher's work first, and their American second-stringers chorused their approval at second-hand. This is not to minimize the merit of his films, merely to stress that there was a great deal of luck in his critical success. His films happened to come at a time when that budgetary classification of Western was getting a wider play and receiving the benefit of press shows and critical attention. A few years earlier, with the same kind of exposure, the films of Lesley Selander might also have received serious critical coverage.

Rio Grande (Republic, 1950), directed by John Ford; with John Wayne, Maureen O'Hara

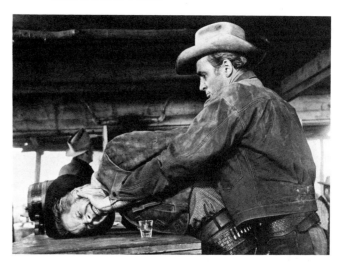

Winchester 73 (Universal, 1950), directed by Anthony Mann; with James Stewart, Dan Duryea

The Outriders (MGM, 1950): Joel McCrea, Ramon Novarro, Barry Sullivan

John Ford's *The Wagonmaster,* made after two big Indian-Cavalry epics, was clearly a "little" picture that he wanted to do, and which allowed him his usual breathing period. It was a minor, very personal film that didn't have to top the big ones that had preceded it. This was a policy that he followed as often as he could, and these commercially minor films often turned out to be among his best. *The Wagonmaster* was a simple, poetic, apotheosis of Ford. Alan Mowbray's Shakespearean ham returned from *My Darling Clementine,* the Clantons from that film turned up too, this time in the persons of an outlaw who was also a religious fanatic, and his brood of half-wit sons; Joanne Dru and Ben Johnson (one of Ford's best and most likeable heroes) were reincarnations of Wayne and Trevor from *Stagecoach,* and Ward Bond, Jane Darwell, Francis Ford (as another lovable wreck of a drunk), Jim Thorpe, and Harry Carey, Jr., also repeated traditional roles. It is a lovely, leisurely movie, full of a romanticized reincarnation of the pioneer spirit, all beautiful images and stirring ballads. Photographically, it is extremely simple. The camera moves only once or twice in the entire film, and never when a lesser director would have made it move to underline a shot. Ford even resists the temptation to track his camera in the breathtaking twilight shots of the women wearily marching along in the dust behind their wagons. They come—and go—while the camera remains static and the audience stays a spectator to the march of history, not a participant in it. (Of course, when Ford *wants* to involve his audience emotionally or dramatically, as in *Stagecoach,* he knows just how to do it. But *The Wagonmaster* was a fond, nostalgic look backward. It was all that Ford wanted, and an emotional involvement, or the omnipresence of a Hollywood camera crew as suggested by elaborate tracking shots, would have spoiled that viewpoint.)

The casually misused label "adult Western" is of course an almost meaningless one. There have *always* been adult Westerns. Too often the phrase, or its substitute, "psychological Western," are convenient escape hatches when by accident a Western turns out to have none of the ingredients deemed necessary to make it a popular success. Television's constant use of the term has made it especially empty. But if any films can be considered to have instituted trends in "adult" Westerns, then they are two related films of the early fifties: *The Gunfighter* from 1950, and *High Noon* from two years later. By far the better of the two films, *The Gunfighter* enjoyed only moderate critical and public success, and was so misunderstood and underrated by its distributors that it was sold as a regluar action Western, its trailer

Ambush (MGM, 1950), with Robert Taylor and Arlene Dahl

Broken Arrow (20th Century- Fox, 1950), directed by Delmer Daves; with Jeff Chandler, Debra Paget, James Stewart

High Lonesome (Eagle-Lion, 1950), with John Barrymore, Jr.

Crooked River (Lippert, 1950), with Russell Hayden and James Ellison

Bells of Coronado (Republic, 1950): The Roy Rogers Westerns became increasingly modern, with airplanes, helicopters, atomic missiles!

Across the Wide Missouri (MGM, 1951), directed by William Wellman; with Clark Gable and Maria Elena Marques

Silver City Bonanza (Republic, 1951), with Rex Allen and Mary Ellen Kay

South of Caliente (Republic, 1951), with Roy Rogers

Dakota Lil (20th Century-Fox, 1951): John Emery, Marie Windsor, George Montgomery

Fort Dodge Stampede (Republic, 1951), with Allan Lane

Valley of Fire (Columbia, 1952) with Gene Autry and Gail Davis

cunningly pulling together its sparse elements of action, slapping on a blood and thunder musical score (the film itself is almost devoid of music, and effectively so), and generally making it look like any one of a thousand other Westerns. In *The Gunfighter* and its many follow-ups, with the theme of a young hoodlum out to make his reputation by killing a wanted man, sympathy has always been with the older outlaw (whose crimes have taken place before the start of the film) and never with the younger would-be gunfighter, who is invariably depicted as sadistic and maladjusted. While this whitewashes the older outlaw, especially as he is also presented as a man weary of killing, aware that he is doomed, at the same time violence for glory's sake and the taking of the law into one's own hands are heartily condemned. But in essence, one *is* asked to sympathize with a killer, and to reject a man whose actions, if not his motives, will benefit society! It is to the film's credit that one never quite realizes this until long afterwards. Beautifully acted and designed (there is just the right, but not overdone, hopeless droop to Gregory Peck's moustache), literate in its writing, incisive in its bursts of action, and superbly photographed by Arthur Miller (carefully avoiding the romantic warmth of his films for John Ford), *The Gunfighter* creates such a mood of inexorable Greek Tragedy that no matter how many times one sees it, one is always hoping subconsciously for that accidental change of circumstance or timing that will bring about a happy ending. The false and romanticized fadeout shot excepted, *The Gunfighter* is a major classic among Western movies.

High Noon, which has usurped so much of the reputation and innovational credit that rightly belongs to King's film, was parlayed into a huge box-office success partly because it *is,* within limits, a very good movie, partly because of the exploitation value of its theme song (a much less common film-plugging gimmick then), and largely because it brought an Academy Award-winning comeback to its popular hero, Gary Cooper, who had been wasted in unimportant films for several years. Historians of the West dislike the film because they insist that in essential details it is false, and that the ballad especially is both an artifice and an anachronism. Critics tended to be misled, giving far too much credit to producer Kramer (whose achievements have never matched his intentions) and director Fred Zinneman (never really at home with such thoroughly American subjects), too little to star Cooper and editor Elmo Williams. However, its twin themes of civic responsibility in a crisis and latent courage in non-heroic citizens (even if rather negatively and pessimistically presented here) soon became absorbed into such subsequent Westerns as *At Gunpoint,* and were rapidly accepted as "new" clichés. Its pessimistic commentary on citizenry's attitude towards non-involvement proved to be sadly prophetic in purely contemporary terms—although in the Westerns themselves one often felt sorry for the outlaws, suddenly beset by an outnumbering group of petty, vengeful townspeople!

The proverbial "shot in the arm" that *High Noon* provided the Western was followed up less than a year later with a booster shot in *Shane.* While clearly it *is* a milestone film, if not a permanent classic, it is a film of diminishing returns and each viewing tends to leave one liking it a little less. (Perhaps it should be stressed that this is not a generally held viewpoint.) Preceded by a reputation that classed it as a white elephant, a production that had gone spectacularly overboard in budget and shooting schedules, it rapidly proceeded to startle Paramount by achieving both critical acclaim and box-office blockbuster stature. After the onslaught of psychological, introspective Westerns that sought to cash in on the success of *High Noon,* it was a refreshing and classic return to the themes of man *vs.* man and man *vs.* nature in the building of the West. With its stunning color photography of the Grand Tetons location, its "class" production, its cast, and sufficient action to satisfy those who didn't care about "class," it could hardly miss. It had the misfortune to go into release in the midst of the nation-wide conversion to wide screens. George Stevens' meticulously composed frames were hacked and elongated in order that *Shane* might open at the Radio City Music Hall as a totally up-to-date production and be sold subsequently as a wide-screen attraction. Even this boomeranged to the film's favor, enlisting the support and sympathy of movie purists (a term not used scornfully) who otherwise might not have been concerned. Yet it is a film that makes its greatest impact the first time around—unless, of course, one has only seen it on television, in which case the vistas that suddenly unfurl on a large theatre screen and in color make a second viewing a genuine revelation. Much of it holds up extremely well as *film;* the photography obviously, the attention to detail, the realism of the simple sets, the ritualistic sadism of Jack Palance's killer, the astounding impact of the shooting of Elisha Cook, Jr. After seeing good guys and bad guys by the thousand crumpling comfortably into the dust through thirty years of "B" Westerns, this sudden confrontation with the physical force of death comes as quite a shock, as Stevens rightly intended. But the film as a total entity now no longer seems to have the strength of these individual components, and the wonder is that its flaws were not apparent long ago. While the film rescued Alan

Examples of increasing economies in the "B" Western

The outlaw gangs reduced to a standard three men (Riley Hill, Marshall Reed, Lee Roberts)

Skimpy "exterior" sets

Skimpier "interior" sets

Ladd from decline and made him a star again, his performance is still the weakest in the film when it should be the strongest, nor is he helped by a pretty buckskin costume which lacks the dramatic showmanship of Palance's costume or the unvarnished realism of the farmers' clothing. Victor Young's score is melodic and easy to remember, but it is incurably romantic and parallel scenes in this film and *The Gunfighter* work much better in the latter without musical backing.

And for all of the use of landscape and superb locations, all that is achieved is an effect of men dwarfed by nature or at war with it. The sense of man's *relationship* to the land—an inherent part of almost any John Ford Western—is almost totally lacking, though there is an acknowledgment of the need for that relationship in the sequence of the uprooting of the tree stump. Perhaps, in essence, this (personal) dissatisfaction with *Shane* today boils down to the difference between Ford and Stevens. Stevens is a meticulous craftsman: he pre-plans, plans again, experiments, discards, shoots endlessly, amasses miles of footage, until he has achieved a kind of mechanical perfection (and there is certainly an art and a skill in that too) and then, in the time that it would take Ford to shoot two cavalry epics, sits down to cut it to a preconceived mathematical pattern. The first time

one sees it (and admittedly, buffs apart, films are really designed to be seen but once) its perfection takes one's breath away. But thereafter one notices more and more the coldness, the lack of the warmth that comes from the unplanned "bit of business" dreamed up spontaneously. Ford often likes to slow his Westerns down and just mark time while he experiments with a specific act or movement: Fonda as Wyatt Earp in *My Darling Clementine,* sitting on a chair on the veranda, balancing himself by moving his feet, is a typical example. This "extraneous" warmth and spontaneity is what makes the Ford Westerns, for all their occasional crudities, so durable. *Stagecoach* and *My Darling Clementine* get better with each viewing; *Shane,* alas, does not, and it is perhaps no coincidence that *Shane's* best performance comes from Ford protégé and player Ben Johnson.

While the deluxe Western of the early fifties was obviously in fine shape, both artistically and commercially, the lot of the humble "B" was far less happy. They were costing more and more to make—and were proving less and less profitable. In the thirties, a decent "B" Western could be made for $20,000 or less. Now they were costing $50,000—and even holding to that price meant such corner-cutting that the resultant quality was low. Action was cheaply staged, and borrowed as much foot-

High Noon (United Artists, 1952, directed by Fred Zinneman, with Gary Cooper

208

Shane (Paramount, 1953), directed by George Stevens

Shane: Jean Arthur, Van Heflin, Brandon de Wilde, Alan Ladd

Shane

209

age from earlier Westerns as possible. Even a single stunt in an Allan Lane Western at Republic might be compiled from as many as three different sources: an establishing scene from a Three Mesquiteers Western perhaps, Gene Autry or John Wayne supplying the next vital bit of action, Allan Lane cut in via a studio-filmed insert, and yet another star in a fourth bit of action to wind it up! Matching and continuity were hardly taken into consideration, and the bigger action sequences were re-used so frequently that even the uninitiated recognized them instantly. Newly filmed action became ultra-standardized. The old-time outlaw gang had now shrunk to a mere three riders; running inserts were always shot on the same stretches of road and cut in regardless of the other locales in use; studio "exteriors" got skimpier, with a few papier-mâché rocks, a bush or two, and much back-projection substituting for decent art-direction. In order to minimize the number of camera set-ups and speed production, dialogue scenes were shot in long uninterrupted takes, without change of angle, camera position, or interpolated close-ups to add variety or dramatic emphasis. RKO Radio did maintain a high

standard to the end with its Tim Holt series, but they had to pay for it in uneconomical budgets that went far beyond even the $50,000 mark. Even in the face of this depression, a few new series were started, and in their initial enthusiasm, offered lively and well above-average Westerns. Republic's Rex Allen series benefitted from Allen's own likeable personality, and expert direction by William Witney, who put astonishing vigor into Westerns like *The Last Musketeer* through sheer pace and free use of the mobile camera trucks in his chase sequences.

At a time when most Westerns were cutting down on action content, the Rex Allens were to be commended for going all-out in their staging of imaginative and expensive action sequences. Monogram, in the process of changing itself into Allied Artists and concentrating on a higher-bracket product, also started an intelligent and interesting new series with Bill Elliott. *The Longhorn, Kansas Territory, Waco,* and *Fargo* provided a very satisfying mixture of good action and good scripts, while *Topeka* (like the others with a story very much in the Bill Hart vein) went suddenly berserk with the mov-

Shane: Elisha Cook, Jr., Jack Palance

The Naked Spur (MGM, 1953), directed by Anthony Mann: James Stewart, Robert Ryan, Janet Leigh, Ralph Meeker, Millard Mitchell

The Man From the Alamo (Universal, 1953), with Glen Ford

The Last Outpost (Paramount, 1953), with Ronald Reagan, Rhonda Fleming

Ride Vaquero (MGM, 1953), with Ava Gardner, Robert Taylor, Anthony Quinn

Tumbleweed (Universal, 1953), with Audie Murphy

Jack Slade (Allied Artists, 1953): Barton MacLane, Mark Stevens, Dorothy Malone

ing camera. On tracks and on a crane, it delved into stagecoaches, circled poker players in dizzying movements, zoomed upwards to catch long-shot action. Not since the German-inspired films of the late twenties had the camera moved so much purely for its own sake, and possibly *never* so much in a Western. Unquestionably the most interesting aspect of this series was the realistic quality of the hero's personal conduct. While Elliott remained essentially a man of integrity, at the same time he upset many of the Boy Scout behavior codes by which most of the cowboy heroes had abided since Tom Mix's day. Foremost among these of course was a taboo on alcoholic drinking; the standard Western hero often had to go to extreme lengths to justify his presence in a saloon, and had to act out in unsubtle pantomime his act of only pretending to drink—lest the villain immediately deduce from his abstinence that he was a Texas Ranger. The hero's refusal to drink anything stronger than sarsaparilla was, of course, one of the standard causes of many a saloon fight. Elliott drank the hard stuff whenever it seemed logical for him to do so—and in fairness to him, he frequented restaurants too, something that other cowboy heroes rarely seemed to find necessary! When he played an outlaw, or a reformed outlaw, he was just that—not a lawman posing as a bad guy, or an orphan adopted and raised by outlaws against his will. While just, he could also be ruthless, selfish, and even unsportsmanlike, sufficiently sensible not to mind holding a gun on an unarmed opponent and beating the truth out of him if the circumstances warranted. This added dimension came too late to have much effect on the "B" Western, but it is interesting that this innovation should arrive via the "B"; the heroes of the "A" Westerns were still basically hewing to the traditional code of behavior at this time, and it wasn't until later that the Widmarks and the Waynes followed in Elliott's realistic, if not salutary, footsteps.

The care lavished on the first Elliotts soon petered out, however, and the last entries in the series were short in length, short on action, and low on good stories and production values. One by one, the series Westerns dropped by the wayside. Johnny Mack Brown, Rex Allen, Tim Holt, Whip Wilson, Bill Elliott, Allan Lane, Monte Hale, Roy Rogers, Gene Autry, Charles Starrett, all making "B" series in 1950, had stopped by 1954. In New York, it was possible to follow their demise week by week at a Times Square theatre that for years had shown nothing but Westerns. At first it had done a solid week's business by coupling two of the best current Westerns; gradually it was forced to take two of anything it could get, then one Western plus some other "B" picture, by

Rebel City (Allied Artists, 1953), with Bill Elliott, Marjorie Lord

Apache (United Artists, 1954), with Burt Lancaster

Bad Day at Black Rock (MGM, 1954), directed by John Sturges; a contemporary Western: Robert Ryan, Spencer Tracy, Ernest Borgnine

Broken Lance (20th Century-Fox, 1954), directed by Edward Dmytryk, a remake of the non-Western *House of Strangers;* Spencer Tracy, Katy Jurado, Richard Widmark

Seven Angry Men (Allied Artists, 1954): Raymond Massey repeating as John Brown

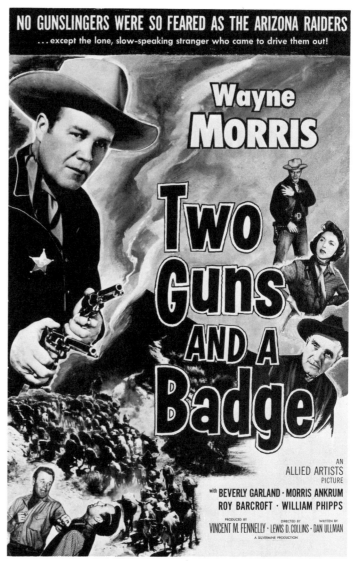

Cowboy (Lippert, 1954), a documentary directed by Elmo Williams

NO GUNSLINGERS WERE SO FEARED AS THE ARIZONA RAIDERS
...except the lone, slow-speaking stranger who came to drive them out!

Wayne **MORRIS**

Two Guns AND A Badge

AN ALLIED ARTISTS PICTURE

with BEVERLY GARLAND · MORRIS ANKRUM
ROY BARCROFT · WILLIAM PHIPPS

PRODUCED BY VINCENT M. FENNELLY · DIRECTED BY LEWIS D. COLLINS · WRITTEN BY DAN ULLMAN
A SILVERMINE PRODUCTION

Wichita (Allied Artists, 1955), directed by Jacques Tourneur; Keith Larsen (as Bat Masterson) and Joel McCrea (as Wyatt Earp)

Two Guns and a Badge (Allied Artists, 1954): last of the "B" series Westerns. Economies extend even to this ad, which includes a stock still from *Cow Country*.

The Spoilers (Universal, 1955), with Jeff Chandler, Rory Calhoun

Run for Cover (Paramount, 1955), with James Cagney, Viveca Lindfors

The Return of Jack Slade (Allied Artists, 1955), with John Ericson

now of such routine interest that it couldn't hope to survive for a week without a third feature being added as a "preview." (The preview was often a thirty-year-old Ken Maynard Western!) Eventually there was nothing left to play, and, rather appropriately, its final Western was Gene Autry's *Last of the Pony Riders*. The last regular "B" Western series to go into production was a good Wayne Morris group for Allied Artists; when the last of those, *Two Guns and a Badge,* went into release in mid-1954, the series Western was dead for good.

Those of us who had grown up on "B" Westerns had often, as children, indulged in masochistic fantasies in which we dreamed that one day, they would be no more. We never really believed that such a dreadful day could ever dawn, for if it did, there would be nothing left to live for. But when that doomsday came (even allowing for the fact that we were by then much older) it wasn't such an impossible thing to live with. Most of our older favorites had died or gone into retirement, and it required no excess of fortitude to say farewell to a Lash LaRue or a Monte Hale. The last of the "B"s were so poor in quality that it was almost better to have no Westerns at all than such pale shadows of former glories. Charles Starrett's "Durango Kid" Westerns at Columbia were being shot in three days, all stock footage, cheap sets and time-consuming low comedy. The fact that many of the stars—William Boyd, Gene Autry, Roy Rogers, Rex Allen—had switched to television was but minor compensation. Although they varied in quality, these TV Westerns, too, were generally substandard. Autry maintained the highest standards, not only in his own Westerns but in the others that his company produced, most notably the actionful *Range Rider* series starring that remarkable stuntman Jock Mahoney. But even these new-style "B"s were to have but a short lifespan before they gave way to the equally standardized but more talky and more "adult" series like *Gunsmoke*. Certainly these were far more elaborately produced than the cheap half-hour shows; *The Lone Ranger,* for example, had been done almost entirely on cramped studio sets, with the same stock riding and exterior scenes cut in once or twice per episode.

Through the years, the big-scale television series Western, graduating to color, name stars, and very occasionally a director of John Ford's stature, improved their scripts and their production values, and worked up popular formats, but no series ever produced a single episode to match a *My Darling Clementine* or a *Gunfighter*. MGM made a rather amusing spoof of the whole television-Western furor, titled *Callaway Went Thattaway*. It zeroed in with some accuracy on the mechanics of merchandising toy guns, hats and other cowboy accessories, and was rather more honest than most Hollywood satires, perhaps because it was satirizing a competitor rather than itself. Nevertheless, it didn't quite have the courage of its own convictions, and after the "End" title came a further long title explaining that it had all been in fun, and that no disrespect was intended to the many cowboy stars who had for so long exhibited civic awareness, social responsibility, and charitable generosity. This added a further touch of irony, since the cowboy stars who really lived up to their responsibilities were rare indeed. Buck Jones was a major exception, but to many of them making Westerns was purely and simply a lucrative business, and at least one Republic Western star of the forties and fifties was so commercially minded, and so consistently egotistical and unpleasant to work with that he was universally hated by all of his directors and co-workers. (Which is doubtless why, unlike Rex Allen, Roy Rogers, and others, his employment since the cessation of his starring series has been almost nil!)

But if the "B" Westerns, bad as they were, were missed, there was some consolation not only in the increased number of "A" Westerns, but also in the way in which they were more and more catering to the action requirements of dyed-in-the-wool Western addicts. Universal worked out an especially satisfying formula: their eighty-minute "A" programmers not only had the star value and the Technicolor production values to enable them to appeal to general audiences, but they had all the slick, fast action of the vanishing "B"s. *The Man from the Alamo* (1953), a Glenn Ford vehicle, had some especially polished stunt work staged and performed by David Sharpe, and in terms of speed and (literally) cliff-hanger action, compared favorably with the best of Republic.

Allied Artists, which had started to make big-budget Westerns in the very late forties with two excellent Rod Cameron vehicles, *Panhandle* and *Stampede,* maintained an interesting schedule through the fifties too. For a medium-budget job, another Rod Cameron film, *Fort Osage,* was quite exceptional: fast, neat, well photographed in Cinecolor and full of well-staged action, all in some seventy minutes. *Shotgun* and *Cow Country* were two other well-above-average Allied Artists Westerns of this period.

Other than for the borrowing of the *High Noon* themes, there were no specific trends during the fifties. A tentative return to the whitewashed badman vehicles never really got past the medium-budget Westerns like *Al Jennings of Oklahoma.* Jennings, one of the last of

Outlaw Treasure (United Artists, 1955), with John Carpenter, Adele Jergens

The Searchers (Warner Brothers, 1956), directed by John Ford; with John Wayne, Ward Bond, Harry Carey, Jr.

Johnny Concho (United Artists, 1956), with Frank Sinatra

The Tall Stranger (Allied Artists, 1957): Virginia Mayo, Michael Ansara

Al Jennings of Oklahoma almost doubled his size to that of Dan Duryea and gave his outlawry the crusading stature of a Jesse James! The renewed activity in the outlaw-biography soon dwindled down to the "B" level, however. While no more series Westerns were made, sporadic "B" Westerns continued to be produced on an individual basis, but usually with color, a minor "name" star, or some exploitation gimmick by which they could gain at least a number of "A"-time playdates. The outlaw vehicle, liberally spaced with violence and sex, proved a useful, though short-lived, type of film in this area, via such cheap and tawdry films as *Outlaw Women* and *The Daltons' Women*.

Boosting the already large numbers of "A" Westerns being turned out in the fifties were the technological changes affecting the movie industry at that time. Three-dimensional films and CinemaScope offered new possibilities to the Western; shooting a Western in Cinema-Scope did not materially increase its budget, but did give it a superficially spectacular aura. 3-D brought added excitement to fight scenes, added depth to chases, but the gimmicks, such as flaming arrows shot "at" the audience, soon became over-familiar. CinemaScope allowed for greater exploitation of landscape and panoramic vistas, although only *White Feather* (1955) took full advantage of this. The good Westerns were usually good in spite of the new processes, not because of them, and many, like *Hondo* (1953), which were shot in 3-D,

the old-time badmen, had himself turned to making two-reel Westerns when he was pardoned in the mid-silent period. Despite being an authentic badman, he rather conspicuously modelled his screen image after William S. Hart, though his films did contain a certain amount of documentary value in showing the day-to-day living pattern of outlaws on the run and the kind of farm and mountain people that befriended them. Columbia's version of his life, however, followed the usual movie pattern: Jennings had been a minor and somewhat inept train robber, and physically was something of a runt.

The Persuader (Allied Artists, 1957)

Gunfight at the OK Corral (Paramount, 1957), directed by John Sturges

Gunfight at the OK Corral: Kirk
Douglas and Burt Lancaster as Doc
Holiday and Wyatt Earp

were actually released in flat versions. *Hondo* was probably the best John Wayne vehicle *not* made by John Ford, and together with Ford's *The Searchers,* stood out among the scores of "A" Westerns produced during the fifties. In terms of quantity, the fifties represented some kind of highpoint for the sustained production of "A" Westerns. Top directors—King Vidor, John Ford, Robert Wise, Jacques Tourneur, Henry Hathaway, Henry King, John Sturges—turned to the Western regularly, while the reigning "name" stars—Gregory Peck, William Holden, Ray Milland, Cornel Wilde, Jeff Chandler, Tyrone Power, Kirk Douglas, Burt Lancaster—made Westerns now as a matter of course, not as a kind of interim novelty.

The end of the fifties could nowhere match the beginning in terms of really first-class Westerns, although in 1958 the veteran Henry Hathaway did come up with a beauty in *From Hell to Texas.* By 1958, the great boom in "A" Westerns had begun to diminish. William Wyler's multi-starred but generally undistinguished *The Big*

The Badge of Marshal Brennan (Allied Artists, 1957), with Jim Davis, Lee Van Cleef

The Oklahoman (Allied Artists, 1957), with Joel McCrea

Man of the West (United Artists, 1958) underlines the violence and sex that have become more prevalent in the Western; Neville Brand, Gary Cooper, Julie London

The Tin Star (Paramount, 1957), with Henry Fonda, Anthony Perkins

The Law and Jake Wade (MGM, 1958): Patricia Owens, Richard Widmark, Robert Taylor, and a glossy MGM "exterior" set

Rio Bravo (Warner Brothers 1959), directed by Howard Hawks: Angie Dickinson and John Wayne

The Left-Handed Gun (Warner Brothers, 1958), directed by Arthur Penn; with Paul Newman

From Hell to Texas (20th Century-Fox, 1958), directed by Henry Hathaway; with Don Murray

The Big Country (United Artists, 1958), directed by William Wyler; Chuck Connors, Gregory Peck, Carrol Baker

Country stole most of the year's thunder. *From Hell to Texas,* with a cast of minor names and a title that suggested a much cheaper kind of picture, was unfortunately lost in the shuffle. This was a pity, for it was not only one of the few Westerns to really use the wide CinemaScope screen creatively, but it was probably also the best Western between Ford's *The Wagonmaster* and Sam Peckinpah's 1962 *Ride the High Country*. The reasons for its success are hard to pin down, since so many factors are involved. The script certainly is a literate and off-beat one, coming up with all the expected action while at the same time avoiding clichéd characters and situations. Even the badmen, as vicious a family as we had seen on the screen since the Clantons

219

STARS OF
TELEVISION WESTERNS

Rory Calhoun with Pat Conway in *The Texan*

Dennis Weaver and James Arness in *Gunsmoke*

Jack Mahoney and Dick Jones in the *Range Rider* series

Guy Madison and Andy Devine (with director Thomas Carr) in the *Wild Bill Hickok* series

(My Darling Clementine) and the Cleggs *(The Wagon-master)*, act with a certain logic and justification, and aren't villains in the usual sense. Don Murray was particularly felicitously cast in the lead—the kind of role that Audie Murphy was always looking for in his Universal Westerns and never quite finding—while Chill Wills, usually given his head by the Johns Ford and Wayne to the detriment of the pictures involved, is not obnoxious here and even quietly effective at times.

Perhaps the biggest surprise of all was that director Hathaway could come up with so different a film. Despite the mysticism of his one really off-beat work, *Peter Ibbetson,* Hathaway has always been a straightforward director of the old school, brought up in the thirties on such films as *Lives of a Bengal Lancer* and the Zane Grey series, continuing into the fifties and sixties with *North to Alaska* and *Five Card Stud.* His one major foray into "serious" Westerns was in Tyrone Power's *Rawhide,* an interesting "mood" and suspense Western of the early fifties.

His films have usually been refreshing and simple, strong on action and visuals, uncluttered by psychology. But in *From Hell to Texas* he seems to have combined the sentiment and austerity of Hart and the slickness and spectacle of Ford. The film has some magnificent outdoor locations—ramshackle towns and single buildings rising starkly out of the dust—that rival those of *Shane.* No decade that began with *The Gunfighter* and *The Wagonmaster* and ended with *From Hell to Texas* can offer much cause for complaint!

The Horse Soldiers (United Artists, 1959), directed by John Ford; with John Wayne and William Holden

The Big Trail (Fox, 1930), with Charlie Stevens, Tyrone Power, Sr., Ian Keith

Somewhere in Sonora (Warner Bros., 1933), with Paul Fix

Stagecoach (United Artists, 1939), with George Bancroft, Claire Trevor

Tall in the Saddle (RKO Radio, 1944), with Harry Woods

New Frontier (Republic, 1939): Winding up his last "B" contract as one of the Three Mesquiteers; with Raymond Hatton, Ray Corrigan

She Wore a Yellow Ribbon (RKO Radio 1949), directed by John Ford; with Victor McLaglen, John Agar, George O'Brien, Arthur Shields

The Commancheros (20th Century-Fox, 1961), with Lee Marvin

True Grit (Paramount, 1969): Henry Hathaway directing Wayne

THE EVOLUTION OF A STAR: JOHN WAYNE

How the West Was Won (MGM, 1962), as General Sherman

223

As a star of independent Westerns in the twenties

As a villain in the thirties (with George Cheseboro)

As the second unit director of Paramount's *Blue* (1969)

As a stuntman/double: in Republic's *Santa Fe Stampede* (1938)

YAKIMA CANUTT:
STAR
TO
DIRECTOR

THE SIXTIES: WESTERNS, WESTERNS EVERYWHERE, BUT...

As these final notes are written, it is sobering, if not downright depressing, to realize that a mere seven months remain of the sixties, and the entire decade has given us only one truly outstanding Western—Sam Peckinpah's *Ride the High Country*—and that at the beginning of the sixties. Westerns in general have tended to stress the age of their protagonists, partly for comedy purposes, but largely from necessity, since many of the bigger Western "names" have aged, and in order to use a sixty-year-old star with some logic, that age has had to be reflected in their story-lines. *Ride the High Country* took Randolph Scott and Joel McCrea (whose physical appearances actually still belied the infirmities that the script attributed to them) as two veteran misfits in a

changing and more lawful West, one trying to perform an honest job with dignity, the other out to make one last haul in order to retire with a measure of comfort. The story had a number of interesting sub-plots and characters and an earthy but tasteful approach to sex. Its strength, however, lay in the sincere and moving portrayals of its stars, and in the beauty and poignancy of its final scene wherein McCrea dies quietly and with the dignity he had sought, as he sinks out of the frame the camera panning over to the rugged Western skyline, emphasizing once more this man's affinity to the land. *Ride the High Country* was not only one of the best Westerns of the sixties, but one of the best from any period. There are those who claim that its success was

225

The Alamo (United Artists, 1960), directed by John Wayne; with Richard Widmark, Laurence Harvey, John Wayne

The Plunderers (Allied Artists, 1960); Ray Stricklyn

The Unforgiven (United Artists, 1960), directed by John Huston; Audrey Hepburn, Lillian Gish

The Misfits (United Artists, 1961), directed by John Huston; Montgomery Clift, Clark Gable

Sergeant Rutledge (Warner Brothers, 1960), directed by John Ford; Woody Strode

The Last Sunset (Universal, 1961): An off-beat Western that included some implied incest; Kirk Douglas, Carol Lynley

Ride the High Country: Ronald Starr, Mariette Hartley, Joel McCrea, Randolph Scott

Ride the High Country (MGM, 1962), directed by Sam Peckinpah

Terror at Black Falls (Beckman Film Corp., 1962)

Lonely Are the Brave (Universal, 1963), with Kirk Douglas

Sergeants Three (United Artists, 1962), with Dean Martin, Frank Sinatra, Peter Lawford

Hud (Paramount, 1962), directed by Martin Ritt; Paul Newman, Brandon de Wilde

The Man Who Shot Liberty Valance (Paramount, 1962), directed by John Ford; Lee Marvin, John Wayne

almost a fluke, in no way attributable to its director, Sam Peckinpah, who was not given sole control over its shooting or editing. And it is true that Peckinpah's subsequent career has been a matter of interesting and unusual misfires, films which have never approached the stature of *Ride the High Country*. But it hardly matters who created its beauty and power; whoever individually or collectively was responsible for it, it has become the best and only truly representative Western of the sixties. The same year (1962) saw another commendably offbeat Western in *Lonely Are the Brave,* in which old-time non-conformist and small-time outlaw Kirk Douglas finds his freedom and his whole way of life menaced first by fences and then by modern technological encroachments. It was an interesting if not wholly successful effort, but seemed pretentious and forced in the face of the simplicity and naturalistic quality of *Ride the High Country*.

John Ford, older, tired, continued to make good Westerns right through the sixties, but much of the old spirit was gone. He became lazy (if a working director in his 70's can be called "lazy"), less of a perfectionist

One Eyed Jacks (Paramount, 1963), directed by and starring Marlon Brando

in his visuals, and shot too much of his films in the studio. Nevertheless, his sincerely felt *Cheyenne Autumn* (despite being badly and inconsistently cut prior to release) would make a graceful and appropriate adieu to the Western film for this old warrior, if indeed it does prove to be his final horse opera.

The more ambitious the Western of the sixties, the more spectacularly it seemed to fail. John Wayne's personally directed *The Alamo* was an overwrought and certainly over-long bore, and Cinerama's *How the West Was Won,* far from being the "definitive" Western it set out to be, was merely a superficial circus, notable for its fine locations, superb photography, and exciting stunt action sequences, but somehow never achieving even conviction, let alone poetry or the genuine epic stature it sought. The most enjoyable Westerns of the sixties tended to be those that aimed at being nothing more than serviceable star vehicles—Howard Hawks' *Eldorado* with John Wayne, for example. Westerns generally seemed to be taking themselves less seriously, to be playing themselves tongue-in-cheek. This mood was accelerated by the unexpected success of *Cat Ballou,* a Jane Fonda vehicle that was such a misfire that it was considered a disaster until someone had the bright idea of a "camp" approach and a selling campaign based on the idea of its being a "put-on" of all Westerns, an idea that—despite the film's occasional good sight-gags—had not been the intention when it was made. Its success prompted even more levity in the Western, extending to 1969's heavy-handed *Support Your Local Sheriff* with James Garner.

But if this tendency to take the Western far less seriously was not very successful, at least it was more enjoyable than the short-lived efforts to take it overseriously. To enjoy a belated "cult" popularity because of its director (Arthur Penn) and star (Paul Newman), 1958's *The Left-Handed Gun,* a Billy the Kid saga, introduced both "method" acting and Broadway stage directorial styles to the West. Undoubtedly the most pretentious and pseudo-poetic Westerns ever made, it even seemed to borrow semi-surrealistic imagery from Luis Buñuel at times! While there certainly should be no rules concerning new approaches to the Western, it seems unlikely that chi-chi theatrics like this can ever work. If there is ever to be "new blood" in the Western, it is more likely to come from established directors who have as yet never ventured into the genre: Orson Welles, Alfred Hitchcock, Stanley Kubrick. Kubrick, significantly, was fired from *One Eyed Jacks* before it was properly under way. Star Marlon Brando took over as director, turning it into a superbly locationed and photographed, but unbearably mannered and ponderous

229

How the West Was Won

film. Quite incidentally, *all* newer Westerns have suffered to a degree from a surfeit of Broadway actors. Most of our old familiar friends: badmen Fred Kohler and Harry Woods, reliable, granite-jawed sheriff Jack Rockwell; the heroine's father, morally strong but physically feeble Lloyd Ingraham or Edward Le Saint; have all gone now. Type-cast they may have been, but their faces merged naturally with Hollywood's West. We knew them and accepted them, and their mere presence im-

230

How the West Was Won (Cinerama, 1964), directed by Henry Hathaway, George Marshall and John Ford

parted a kind of instant realism which the newer breed of character actors cannot duplicate.

Another minor development, worth mentioning in passing, is the very recent exploitation of the Western scene by the makers of the fast-buck "nudie" movies. Lowering of censorship barriers in the mid-sixties opened up a whole new market for the exploitation quickies dealing in unvarnished sex and (usually separately) ferocious sadism. The West, apart from supply-

Outrage (MGM, 1964): the Western remake of *Rashomon;* Claire Bloom, Paul Newman

Outrage: Paul Newman, Laurence Harvey

Four for Texas (Warner Brothers, 1964): Dean Martin, Ursula Andress

Cat Ballou (Columbia, 1965): Stubby Kaye, Jane Fonda, Nat King Cole

The Treasure of Silver Lake (Columbia, 1965), directed by Harold Reinl; one of the new German Westerns starring Lex Barker

How the West Was Won: James Stewart and Carrol Baker

The Hallelujah Trail (United Artists, 1965), directed by John Sturges; with Burt Lancaster, Jim Hutton

Major Dundee (Columbia, 1965), directed by Sam Peckinpah; with Charlton Heston

The Sons of Katie Elder (Paramount, 1965), with John Wayne

The Bounty Killer (Embassy Pictures, 1965), directed by
Spencer Bennet; Audrey Dalton, Richard Arlen

233

Billy the Kid versus Dracula (Embassy Pictures, 1965)

Requiem for a Gunfighter (Embassy Pictures, 1965): veteran Western stars Bob Steele and Tim McCoy on location with producer Alex Gordon

Eldorado (Paramount, 1966), directed by Howard Hawks

ing outdoor locations (cutting down studio costs) and a logical reason for color, also provided plenty of opportunities for sex (rape, nude swims) and violence (ritual and revenge rape, hangings, whippings). 1969's *The Bushwackers* was only one of several such Westerns to run this gamut; during the same year, the "underground" cinema also discovered the West, Andy Warhol's *Lonesome Cowboys* adding degeneracy and artistic vacuity in the name of "experimental" film. However, these cultural affronts can never be considered a serious or major part of the mainstream of the Western.

The one dominant trend of the sixties was the sudden commercial and artistic popularity of the European-made Western. Europe, and specifically Germany, had always made a modicum of home-grown Westerns, and in the thirties and forties Hans Albers, Germany's Clark Gable, cavorted Teutonically in several local horse operas. Spectacularly rising production costs in the fifties and sixties, however, made it economically sound for Hollywood to begin shooting its own Westerns in European locales, but this minor trend was soon taken over by the Germans and the Italians, who began to specialize in their own full-blooded Westerns, taking every Hollywood cliché seriously, enlarging on them, and adding liberal doses of sex and violence. The hybrids that resulted were mixed breeds indeed. The Italian *A Fistful of Dollars* was a careful and precise remake of Kurosawa's Samurai film *Yojimbo,* which itself was a deliberate attempt to adapt the style and visuals of John Ford's Westerns to the Japanese idiom. So popular did the European Westerns become that Hollywood began setting up co-production deals and sending its own stars over, and finally—as in MGM's *Hang 'Em High,* a Clint Eastwood vehicle—shooting Westerns on its own home ground again, but in the new terse, violent, pseudo-realistic style made popular by the Italians. The Germans, on the other hand, falling back on the works of their own Karl May—a homegrown James Fenimore Cooper—embarked on a series of elaborate color specials, all very much in the Hollywood style of the twenties, simplified but undeniably spectacular and full of mass action. Since these genuinely large-scale films could be made for a fraction of the cost of Hollywood Westerns, they made it increasingly difficult for the Hollywood producer to turn out saleable products that could compete with them in the open market. Nevertheless, the Western was too ingrained a part of Hollywood tradition for it ever to be abandoned. John Wayne went on grinding out inexpensive but solid actioners like *The War Wagon,* while an enterprising independent producer, Alex Gordon, in films like *The Bounty Killer* and *Requiem for a Gunfighter,* performed yeoman service to

A Fistful of Dollars (United Artists, 1967): pace-setter for the Italian Western cycle

Custer of the West (Cinerama, 1968), with Robert Shaw (center)

Eldorado: Robert Mitchum, John Wayne

Day of the Evil Gun (MGM, 1968): Arthur Kennedy, Glen Ford

Support Your Local Sheriff (United Artists, 1969): James Garner, Walter Brennan

Blue: Terence Stamp, Joanna Pettit

Custer (20th Century-Fox TV, 1968): Wayne Maunder (left) in an episode from the short-lived TV series

Blue
(Paramount, 1967):
Terence Stamp

tradition and nostalgia by uniting such veteran Western stars as Tim McCoy (still as virile looking in the sixties as he had been in the twenties), Bob Steele, Buster Crabbe, Johnny Mack Brown, Rod Cameron and even the venerable Broncho Billy Anderson, whose bright eyes and striking profile had weathered almost seven decades!

The credits and plots alone of the last Westerns of the sixties reflect the changes that have been taking place. *Once Upon a Time in the West* presents the erstwhile Wyatt Earp and Frank James, Henry Fonda, as a lecherous badman, and is directed by Italy's Serge Leone. *Paint Your Wagon* features a heroine with the thoroughly "mod" idea of maintaining two husbands and an unorthodox male lead in Lee Marvin.

Undoubtedly the most acclaimed, criticized, and certainly the most controversial Western of the decade was 1969's *The Wild Bunch*—curiously enough, directed by Sam Peckinpah, who started the sixties off so promisingly with *Ride the High Country*. Much of *The Wild Bunch* is Peckinpah at his best; the reconstruction of a period, the attention to realistic detail, the boisterous and bawdy comedy (without the slapstick excesses of John Ford), the wry and sad commentary on men, good and bad, who in their own way helped to build a West that is now passing them by. But *The Wild Bunch* also became a kind of paean to violence, and neither the pious pronouncements of its stars and director that it *had* to depict violence graphically in order to condemn it, nor the unquestioned virtuosity of its pictorial style (slaughter scenes and moments of excessively detailed blood-letting presented in slow-motion to create an effect of choreography and ritual) could really counteract or justify the effect of revulsion and nausea that it created.

Inevitably, violence has always been present in the Western in the form of its standard action content, but rarely as little more than a charade. In the "B" Westerns men could be dragged by horses, beaten senseless in fistfights, and shot full of holes, all without a murmur of pain and without a drop of blood showing. Perhaps the high spot of this kind of bloodless brutality was reached in *Wyoming Hurricane*, a Columbia "B" of 1944. In it, hero Russell Hayden subdues villain Paul Sutton after a furious fistic set-to. Neither has a mark on him. Sutton won't give Hayden the information he needs. With markedly unsportsmanlike behavior for a "B" Western hero, Hayden proceeds to shoot his unarmed opponent in an effort to make him talk. After three bullets in the left arm, none of them productive of blood, Sutton decides to talk, Hayden relaxes his vigilance for a moment, and Sutton jumps him. There is another prolonged fight, in which Sutton manages to conceal rather well

Paint Your Wagon: Lee Marvin, Jean Seberg

The Wild Bunch (Warner Bros.-Seven Arts, 1969), directed by Sam Peckinpah

the fact that one arm is riddled with bullets, although this may well have something to do with his ultimately losing the battle. Even for a "B" Western, this kind of stamina and disregard of the most elementary realism was a bit extreme; but in its obsession with violence and in the shock tactics employed, *The Wild Bunch* takes the same kind of charade to the opposite extreme, making it a Western equivalent of those Hammer Frankenstein films in which eyeballs and dismembered limbs are used not to frighten (a difficult feat even for a gifted director) but merely to revolt (the easiest and laziest accomplishment of all).

Yet much of the traditionalist approach remains. One of the more interesting Westerns of 1969, *True Grit,* presents John Wayne—with makeup and costuming that emphasize rather than minimize his years—as an ageing deputy marshal. Based on a novel that was a sixties' best-seller, its opening hour suffers from a possibly too rigid adherence to its source material. Although the Arkansas 1880 period is well and accurately recreated, there is too great an emphasis on "characters," most of them played by method-oriented stage actors with both eyes on the 1970 "Best Supporting Actor" Academy Award. The novel's heroine, Mattie Ross, may have read well, but

Paint Your Wagon (Paramount, 1969): shooting on location

100 Rifles (20th Century-Fox, 1969): Racquel Welch, Burt Reynolds, Jim Brown

Once Upon a Time in the West (Paramount, 1969), directed by Sergio Leone; with Henry Fonda

in the person of mannered and aggressive actress Kim Darby she, in the current vernacular, comes on much too strong, and is forever reminding one of a 1938 Judy Garland looking for an excuse to sing. Fortunately, the second hour of the film switches to its manhunt theme, and maestros Henry Hathaway and John Wayne take over, pushing her (though not quite far enough) into the background where she belongs. Beautifully photographed in breathtaking California and Colorado locations, *True Grit* has only one brief studio "exterior," and while its action content is limited to the closing reels, it is sharp, vicious (admittedly, unnecessarily bloody at times), and expertly staged. Unexpectedly, Wayne, playing some scenes for pure comedy, does some of his best acting in any non-John Ford Western. One scene in which he half humorously, yet half wistfully, describes his brief married life and the son who didn't like him, reveals a subtlety and an honest warmth in Wayne that has rarely been displayed before. *True Grit* will probably be far less acclaimed that the pretentious and derivative *Will Penny* (which couldn't have existed at all had it not been for *The Wagonmaster* and *Shane*), but is a much better picture. It would also make as perfect and graceful a farewell to the Western for Wayne as *Ride the High Country* had been for McCrea and Scott; an ideal climax to an almost forty-year career that had begun with *The Big Trail*. But with Gary Cooper gone, Wayne has not only become Hollywood's Western figurehead, but he is also still a box-office giant. Obviously he will go on making Westerns for as long as his expanding girth can stride a saddle. One can only hope that when he does decide to hang up his boots (if not his political guns!) it will be with a vehicle as sympathetic and felicitous as *True Grit*.

True Grit (Paramount, 1969), directed by Henry Hathaway; with John Wayne

INDEX

Abbot & Costello, 7
Abilene Town, 187
Ace of Clubs, The, 100
Acord, Art, 69, 83, 89
Across the Wide Missouri, 203, 205
The Alamo, 178, 226, 229
Albuquerque, 178
Allegheny Uprising, 174
Al Jennings of Oklahoma, 215, 216
Allen, Bob, 132
Allen, Rex, 141, 205, 210
Along Came Jones, 186
America, 28
Anderson, G. M., 18, 20, 21, 22, 37, 237
Angel and the Badman, The, 188, 190
Apache, 212
Arbuckle, Fatty, 61
Arizona, 113, 175, 177
Arizona Badman, 11, 128
Arizona Bound, 102, 190
Arizona Cyclone, 196
Arizona Mahoney, 139
Arizona Legion, 150
Arizona Whirlwind, 101
The Arizonian, 158
Arlen, Richard, 120, 121, 233
Arness, James, 80, 220
At Gunpoint, 206
Autry, Gene, 4, 8, 126, 137, 146, 169,
    191, 194, 206
Avenger, The, 131

Back Trail, 83
Bad Bascomb, 182
Bad Day at Black Rock, 212
Badge of Marshall Brennan, The, 218
Badlands of Dakota, 188
Badman of Brimstone, The, 154
Badman's Territory, 184
Badmen of Missouri, 182
Baggott, King, 43
Ballew, Smith, 143
Baker, Bob, 127, 139, 140, 143, 148
Bank Robbery, 17, 18
Bar 20 Justice, 135

Bar 20 Rides Again, 139
Barclay, Joan, 144
Barcroft, Roy, 149, 197
Barnes, George, 2, 4
Barry, Red, 190, 193
Barthelmess, Richard, 35
Barton, Buzz, 96
Battle of Elderbush Gulch, The, 27
Battle of the Redmen, The, 31
Beach, Rex, 58
Beauty and the Bandit, 191
Beery, Noah, Sr., 194
Beebe, Ford, 94, 196
Beery, Wallace, 109, 154, 182
Bell, Rex, 126
Belle Starr, 182
Bells of Coronado, 205
Bells of Rosarita, 9, 198
Bennet, Spencer G., 150, 233
Big Country; The, 217, 219
Big Show, The, 9
Big Trail, The, 55, 109, 110, 111,
    114-119, 222
Big Valley, 12
Birth of a Nation, The, 28, 52
Billy the Kid, 109, 159, 181
Billy the Kid vs. Dracula, 234
Black Bandit, The, 143
Black Bart, 183
Blazing Six-Shooters, 195
Blazing the Trail, 28
Boetticher, Bud, 203
Blood on the Moon, 184, 188
Blue, 224, 236
Bogart, Humphrey, 132, 181
Border Brigands, 138, 139
Borzage, Frank, 33, 144
Boyd, William, 8, 97, 126, 133, 134, 139,
    153, 193, 196
Branded, 131
Branding Broadway, 60
Brass Commandments, 89
Braveheart, 96
Breed of the Border, 134
Brigham Young, 178

Broken Arrow, 200, 201, 203, 204
Broken Lance, 213
Broncho Billy and the Baby, 18
Broncho Billy's Christmas Dinner, 21
Broncho Billy's Oath, 21
Bronson, Betty, 98
Bronze Buckaroo, 148
Brown, Johnny Mack, 109, 112, 120,
    158, 191, 193, 196
Buck Benny Rides Again, 176
Buckskin Frontier, 188
Budgets, 208-9
Buffalo Bill, 178
Buffalo Bill, Jr., 84, 129
Bulldog Courage, 137
Bullet Code, 195
Burnette, Smiley, 146
Bushwackers, The, 234

Cagney, James, 181
Cahn, Edward, 118
Calgary Stampede, 91
California, 102, 103, 178
California Mail, 106, 107
Callaway Went Thataway, 214, 215
Cameo of Yellowstone, 61
Cameron, Rod, 186
Campbell, Colin, 65
Canutt, Yakima, 8, 94, 95, 146, 152, 164,
    165, 224
Canyon Passage, 187
Captive of Billy the Kid, 10
Captured, 196
Caravan Trail, The, 198
Carey, Harry, 47, 48, 62, 90, 91, 118,
    143
Carpenter, John, 215
Carre, Bartlett, 138
Carson, Sunset, 190, 192
Cassidy of Bar 20, 138
Cat Ballou, 229, 232
Caught, 121
Chandler, Lane, 98, 170
Chaney, Lon, Jr., 170
Chatterton, Tom, 33

242

Cherokee Strip, 142
Cherokee Strip landrush, 43, 113, 121
Cheyenne Tornado, The, 138
A Child of the Desert, 61
Chip of the Flying U, 65
Cimarron, 43, 113, 114, 115, 121, 122
Circus Ace, The, 89
Clark, Daniel, 67
Cobb, Edmund, 84, 128
Code of the West, 92
Cody, Bill, 98, 101
Coleman, Don, 81
Collins, Lewis D., 196
Colorado Sunset, 146, 147
Colorado Territory, 196
Color processes, 188
Commancheros, The, 223
Conquering Horde, 120
Conquerors, The, 115
Cooper, Gary, 3, 78, 102, 133, 156, 185, 186, 218
Cooper, James Fenimore, 32
Corporal's Daughter, The, 26
Corrigan, Ray, 128
Crosland, Alan, 155
Costuming, 4
Covered Wagon, The, 28, 43, 70-75, 178
Cowboy, 213
Cowboy and the Senorita, The, 151
Cowboy Kid, The, 20
Crabbe, Buster, 9, 139, 140
Crashing Through, 149
Crescent Pictures, 9
Crimson Trail, The, 139
Cripple Creek Bar-room, 14
Crooked River, 205
Cruze, James, 70-75, 155
Custer, 236
Custer, Bob, 90, 96, 97
Custer of the West, 235
Custer's Last Fight, 34
Custer's Last Stand, 170
Cyclone, The, 66
Cyclone of the Saddle, 137

Dakota, 190
Dakota Lil, 206
Dalton Women, The, 216
Dark Command, The, 174, 175, 176
Daves, Delmer, 203
Dawn Rider, The, 136
Day of the Evil Gun, 235
Dean, Eddie, 194
DeMille, Cecil B., 58, 59, 160, 164, 166
Dempster, Carol, 35
The Denver Dude, 102
Deserter, The, 30, 152
Desert Gold, 33, 140
Desmond, William, 57, 63, 138, 194
Desperate Trails, 148, 149

Destry Rides Again, 138, 163, 174
Devil Horse, The, 95
Dew, Eddie, 196
Dix, Richard, 78, 122
Don Quickshot of the Rio Grande, 83
Drums of the Desert, 102
Duel in the Sun, 174, 179, 199
Duncan, Deuce, 63
Dunlap, Scott, 190, 191
Durand of the Badlands, 89
Dwan, Alan, 176

Eagleshirt, William, 25
Earp, Wyatt, 5, 115, 132, 196, 213
Edison Studios, 24
Eldorado, 229, 234, 235
Elliott, Bill, 69, 127, 132, 192, 194, 210, 212
El Paso, 178
Emerson, John, 60
End of the Trail, 130, 134, 139, 155
English, John, 190
Essanay Company, 18
Evans, Dale, 151, 191

Fairbanks, Douglas, 59, 60
Fairbanks, William, 62
Fargo, 210
Farnum, Dustin, 58
Farnum, William, 57, 63, 89, 195
Fighters of the Saddle, 83
Fighting Blood, 26, 28
Fighting Caravans, 133
Fighting Shepherdess, The, 85, 86
Finley, Evelyn, 193
Finney, Edward, 150, 194
Fistful of Dollars, A, 234, 235
Five Card Stud, 221
Flaming Bullets, 198
Flaming 40's, The, 90
Flaming Frontier, The, 77, 78
Flynn, Errol, 176
Foran, Dick, 138, 142
Forbidden Trails, 190
Ford, Francis, 30, 32, 49, 204
Ford, John, 9, 16, 44, 46-56, 70-75, 166, 172, 173, 178, 196, 199, 201, 204, 208, 229
Fort Apache, 52
Forlorn River, 99
Fort Dodge Stampede, 206
Four Faces West, 188
Four for Texas, 231
Frazee, Jane, 7
Fritz, 38
From Hell to Texas, 217, 219, 221
Frontier Badmen, 184
Frontier Gal, 175
Frontier Marshal, 10, 159
Fugitive Sheriff, The, 5
Fuller, Sam, 203
Fury at Furnace Creek, 178

Gable, Clark, 119, 120, 226
Galloping Cowboy, 98
Galloping Jinx, The, 97
Gay Cavalier, The, 197
Gentle Annie, 178
Gentleman from Texas, The, 191
Geronimo, 175, 178
Gibson, Hoot, 47, 54, 77, 80, 81, 83, 91, 92, 102, 141, 190, 193
Girl of the Golden West, The, 154, 160
Gish, Dorothy, 59
Gish, Lillian, 27, 104, 199, 226
Goddess of Sagebrush Gulch, The, 26, 27, 28
Gold Is Where You Find It, 176
God's Country and the Woman, 155
Golden Trail, The, 195
Goodwill Productions, 95
Gordon, Alex, 234
Gordon of Ghost City, 139
Go West, 93, 176
Grant, Kirby, 195
Great Barrier, The, 72
Great K & A Train Robbery, The, 67
Great Man's Lady, The, 177
Great Meadow, The, 120
Great Train Robbery, The, 2, 4, 14, 15
Green, Alfred E., 188
Grey Devil, The, 101
Grey Vulture, The, 83
Grey, Zane, 8, 32, 58, 66, 78, 132, 133, 155, 191
Griffith, David W., 23-27, 36, 37, 52, 58, 59
Gunfight at the OK Corral, The, 11, 217
Gunfighter, The, 181, 200, 202, 204, 206
Gunman from Bodie, The, 190
Gun Packer, 145
Gunsmoke, 214
Gunsmoke Trail, 10

Hale, Monte, 192
Hallelujah Trail, The, 232
Hang 'Em High, 234
Hanging at Jefferson City, The, 20
Hangman's House, 47
Harlem Rides the Range, 148
Hart, Neal, 62
Hart, William S., 3, 6, 17, 37, 39-43, 57, 60, 69, 109, 112, 132, 133
Hathaway, Henry, 217, 221
Hatton, Dick, 81, 100
Hatton, Raymond, 190, 191
Hawks, Howard, 200
Hayden, Russel, 193, 194, 237
Hayes, George, 151, 191, 192
Hayworth, Rita, 142
Hazards of Helen, The, 57
Heart of the Golden West, 152
Heart of the North, 155
Heart of the Rockies, 11, 146
Heir to Trouble, 12

Hello Cheyenne, 67
Hell's Heroes, 111
Hell's Hinges, 39, 40, 41, 66
High Lonesome, 205
High Noon, 3, 204, 206, 208
His Bitter Pill, 61
Hillyer, Lambert, 38, 130, 191
Holiday, Doc, 10, 11, 18
Hollywood Cowboy, 9
Hollywood Roundup, 9
Holmes, Helen, 57
Holt, Jack, 69, 76, 78, 139
Holt, Tim, 199
Holy Terror, The, 131
Hondo, 216
Honky Tonk, 177
Honor of the Range, 138
Hoodoo Ann, 61
Horse Soldiers, The, 54, 221
Howard, William K., 76, 78, 102, 105
Hopalong Cassidy, 133, 161
How the West Was Won, 223, 229, 230
Hoxie, Al, 81, 100
Hoxie, Jack, 82, 83
Humes, Fred, 81, 84
Hud, 228
Huston, John, 203, 226

Idaho, 151
I Killed Wild Bill Hickok, 164
Ince, Thomas H., 23-27, 30-33, 152
Indian Agent, 199
Indian Massacre, The, 31, 33, 83
Indians Are Coming, The, 109
In Early Arizona, 132
In Old Arizona, 109
In Old Cheyenne, 197
In Old Monterey, 10, 146
In Old Oklahoma, 186, 190
In Old Sacramento, 69
Iron Horse, The, 43, 51, 54
It Happened in Hollywood, 9, 253

Jack McCall Desperado, 164
Janice Meredith, 86
Jeffries, Herb, 148
Jennings, Al, 17, 215
Jerry and the Gunman, 60
Jesse James, 55, 78, 83, 105, 178, 180, 181
Johnny Concho, 215
Jones, Buck, 4, 8, 51, 81, 89, 91, 125, 130, 131, 138, 139, 190, 191
Just Tony, 67

Kansan, The, 186
Kansas Pacific, 72
Kansas Territory, 210
Karloff, Boris, 129
Kramer, Stanley, 206
Kay, Mary Ellen, 205
Keene, Tom, 109, 140, 142, 193

Keith of the Border, 63
Kerrigan, J. Warren, 57
Kimbrough, John, 191
King, Henry, 59, 180, 206
King of the Bandits, 199
King of the Mounties, 171
King of the Rodeo, 86
Kit Carson, 180
Knight, Fuzzy, 148
Knickerbocker Buckaroo, 61
Kohler, Fred, 6, 138, 230
Kohler, Fred, Jr., 137
Kubrick, Stanley, 229
Kyne, Peter B., 18

Lane, Allan, 192
Lang, Fritz, 176, 178
Last Drop of Water, The, 25, 28
Last, The, 113
Last Frontier, The, 97
Last Musketeer, The, 210
Last Outlaw, The, 158
Last Outpost, The, 211
Last Roundup, The, 194
Lawless Valley, 140
Last of the Duanes, The, 63, 191
Law of the 45s, 125, 137
Last of the Mohicans, The, 88, 169
Last of the Pony Riders, The, 214
Last Sunset, The, 226
Law and Jake Wade, The, 218
Law and Order, 112, 115, 123
Lawless Code, 199
Law of the Range, The, 90
Law West of Tombstone, The, 143
Lease, Rex, 137
Lewis, Joseph H., 139, 196
Lightning Bill, 129
Little, Ann, 33
Little Train Robbery, The, 16
Livingston, Bob, 128, 144
Lloyd, Frank, 72, 165
Loaded Pistols, 194
London, Tom, 169
Lonely Are the Brave, 228, 229
Lone Ranger, The, 170
Lonesome Cowboys, 234
Lone Star Ranger, The, 67, 194
Longhorn, The, 210
Loos, Anita, 60
Lucky Larkin, 109
Luden, Jack, 132, 144
Lugosi, Bela, 88
Lyons, Cliff, 135, 190

MacDonald, William Colt, 125, 141
McCoy, Tim, 72, 82, 90, 100, 102, 109, 125, 130, 137, 144, 190, 234
McCrea, Joel, 188, 225
McRae, Henry, 105
McDonald, Wallace, 86, 168

Madison, Guy, 220
Mahoney, Jock, 220
Major Dundee, 232
Maloney, Leo, 84, 94, 95
Man from Death Valley, The, 129
Man from Hell's Edges, The, 8
Man from Music Mountain, The, 152
Man from the Alamo, The, 211, 215
Manhattan Madness, 61
Man of Conquest, 165, 178, 180
Man of Nerve, A, 90
Man of the Forest, 133, 134
Man of the West, 218
Man Who Shot Liberty Valance, The, 55, 228
Martyrs of the Alamo, 58
Marked Men, 50
Mascot Pictures, 140
Massacre, 155
Massacre, The, 28
Massacre River, 13
Karl, May, 234
Maunder, Wayne, 236
Maynard, Ken, 12, 82, 86, 90, 94, 95, 106, 107, 109, 138, 146, 193
Maynard, Kermit, 126, 128
Men of Texas, 184, 186
Michigan Kid, The, 104
Miller, Arthur, 206
Miller, Walter, 5, 6, 139, 168, 170
Miracle Rider, The, 169
Misfits, The, 226
Mitchum, Robert, 191
Mix, Ruth, 69
Mix, Tom, 20, 43, 62-69, 109, 132, 138, 139, 169
M'liss, 60, 64
Monogram Pictures, 152, 190, 191
Montgomery, George, 191
Moonlight on the Prairie, 11
Moore, Colleen, 66, 87
Moran, Peggy, 197
Morris, Chester, 8
Mulford, Clarence E., 133
Murietta, Joaquin, 126, 129
Murphy, Audie, 203, 221
Musical Westerns, 148
My Darling Clementine, 178, 196, 199, 208
My Pal the King, 132, 138

Naked Spur, The, 211
Narrow Trail, The, 43
Near the Trail's End, 130
Negro Westerns, 148
Nevada, 100
Neumann, Harry, 153
New Frontier, The, 222
Newill, James, 148
Night Cry, The, 96
North of '36, 78
North of the Rio Grande, 142

North West Mounted Police, 166, 174, 178
North West Passage, 178
Nugget Nell, 59

O'Brian, Hugh, 80
O'Brien, George, 8, 128, 131, 132, 140, 150, 191
O'Day, Nell, 193, 196
Oklahoma Kid, The, 176, 180
Oklahoman, The, 218
Old Chisholm Trail, The, 197
Once Upon a Time in the West, 237, 240
One Eyed Jacks, 229
One Hundred Rifles, 240
On the Night Stage, 38
Open Range, 98
Outcasts of Poker Flat, The, 49, 50
Outlaw, The, 175, 183, 199
Outlaws of Sonora, 144, 146
Outlaw Treasure, 215
Outlaw Women, 216
Outrage, 231
Outriders, The, 203
Overland Mail, 170
Ox Bow Incident, The, 105, 115, 187, 196

Painted Desert, The, 119, 120
Painted Stallion, 169
Paint Your Wagon, 237, 238, 239
Panamint's Badman, 143
Partners of the Trail, 162
Past Redemption, 33
Peckinpah, Sam, 219, 225, 227, 229, 237
Perils of Pauline, 167
Perrin, Jack, 101, 105
Persuader, The, 216
Phantom Bullet, The, 86
Phantom Empire, The, 146, 169
Phantom Plainsmen, The, 10
Phantom Ranger, The, 10, 144
Phantom Rider, The, 139
Pickford, Mary, 59, 64
Pine-Thomas Productions, 178
Pinto Ben, 3
Pioneer Days, 100
Pioneer Scout, The, 104
Plainsman, The, 156, 161, 164
Plainsman and the Lady, The, 69, 188
Plunderers, The, 226
Pony Express, The, 74, 76
Pony Express Rider, The, 65
Porter, Edwin S., 14, 15, 71
Powdersmoke Range, 158
Prairie Pirate, The, 94
Producers Releasing Corp., 194
Puritan Pictures, 9
Pursued, 196

Race for Millions, A, 16, 18, 19
Racketeers of the Range, 140

Rainbow Trail, The, 67
Ramona, 25, 154
Ramrod, 188
Randall, Jack, 127, 152
Ranchlife in the Great South West, 64
Range Busters, The, 190, 191
Range Defenders, 146
Range Law, 65
Range Rider, 214
Rangers of Fortune, 178, 184
Rawhide, 221
Rebel City, 212
Rebellion, 142
Red Raiders, The, 86, 90
Red Rider, The, 139
Red River, 12, 179, 200
Red River Valley, 137
Renegade Trail, 153
Republic Pictures, 7, 8, 69, 140, 146
Requiem for a Gunfighter, 234
Rescued from an Eagle's Nest, 25
Return of Jack Slade, 213
Reynolds, Lyn, 66
Reynolds, Marjorie, 143
Rhodes, Rocky, 139
Ride 'Em Cowboy, 7, 176
Ride Ranger Ride, 146
Ride the High Country, 219, 225, 226, 227, 229
Ride Vaquero, 146
Ridin' Down the Canyon, 10
Ridin' the Wind, 91
Ridin' Tornado, The, 130
Riders of the Dawn, 153
Riders of the Desert, 125
Riders of the Purple Sage, 66, 191, 197
Riders of the Rockies, 10
Rin Tin Tin, 96
Rio Bravo, 219
Rio Grande, 203
Rio Rita, 113
Ritter, Tex, 151, 194
Roaring West, The, 139
Robbers' Roost, 134
Robin Hood of Eldorado, 154, 157
Rogell, Al, 86
Rogers, Roy, 5, 7, 141, 148, 151-153, 191
Rogers, Will, 61, 68
Roland, Ruth, 166
Roll Wagons Roll, 151
Romance of the Redwoods, 60
Roosevelt, Buddy, 85, 97
Rose Marie, 154, 157
Rosson, Arthur, 161
Roughshod, 189
Roundup, The, 61
Ruggles, Wesley, 113, 177
Run for Cover, 214
Run of the Arrow, 203
Russel, Reb, 138
Russel, William, 59

Saddle Tramp, 188
Salome, Where She Danced, 186
San Antonio, 177
Santa Fe Stampede, 224
Santa Fe Trail, 175-6
Santschi, Tom, 58
Scarlet Days, 35, 36
Scott, Fred, 148
Scott, Randolph, 159, 225
Searchers, The, 215
Secrets, 59, 114, 155
Seitz, George B., 180
Selander, Lesley, 90, 190, 203
Selig Company, 20, 64
Señor Daredevil, 94
Sergeant Rutledge, 226
Sergeants Three, 228
Serials, 167
Seven Angry Men, 213
Seven Men from Now, 203
Shane, 207-209, 241
Sheriff's Love, The, 18
Sherman, George, 203
Sherman, Harry, 161, 188
She Wore a Yellow Ribbon, 201, 223
Shooting High, 9
Sierra Sue, 10, 148
Silver City Bonanza, 205
Silver Spurs, 152
Singer Jim McKee, 43
Singing Vagabond, The, 146
Six Cylinder Love, 65
Sky High, 67
Sky Pilot, 72, 87
Sloane, Paul, 178
Small Town Idol, 6, 61
Smith, Cliff, 83
Slade, Jack, 77,
Smoking Guns, 136, 138
Somewhere in Sonora, 222
Sons of Katie Elder, The, 233
South of Caliente, 205
South of the Border, 146
South of the Chisholm Trail, 198
Spoilers, The, 58, 112, 113, 184, 214
Squawman, The, 58
Stagecoach, 16, 44, 49, 52, 53, 153, 163, 166, 172, 174, 196, 222
Stagecoach Driver and the Lady, The, 65
Stalking Moon, The, 237
Stampede, 189
Stand Up and Fight, 160
Starret, Charles, 127, 131, 132, 194
Steele, Bob, 8, 83, 125, 130, 134, 234
Stevens, Charles, 170
Stevens, George, 207
Stewart, Anita, 85, 86
Stewart, Roy, 57, 63
Straight Shooting, 47-50, 54
Streets of Laredo, 160, 189
Struss, Karl, 133
Sturges, John, 196, 212

Sullivan, C. Gardner, 28, 40
Sundown Jim, 194
Sunrise, 67
Support Your Local Sheriff, 229, 235
Sutter's Gold, 71, 155, 156
Sweet, Blanche, 26
Swifty, 141

Tall in the Saddle, 184, 222
Tall Stranger, The, 216
Tall T, The, 203
Taylor, Ray, 196
Terhune, Max, 128
Terror at Black Falls, 228
Testing Block, The, 40, 41
Texans, The, 159-160, 165
Texan, The, 220
Texas, 177
Texas Rangers, The, 156, 159, 160-1
Texas Rangers Ride Again, The, 184
Texas Trail, 135
Thompson, Fred, 81, 91, 104
Three Badmen, 54, 77
Three Godfathers, 8, 9, 156, 189
Three Mesquiteers, The, 128, 141, 146, 190, 222
Three Word Brand, 41
They Died with Their Boots On, 176
Thundering Herd, 76, 133
Thunder Trail, 133
Tides of Empire, 106
Tin Star, The, 218
Toll of the Desert, 128, 137
Topeka, 210
de Toth, André, 188
To The Last Man, 8, 133
Trail Beyond, The, 152
Trail Blazers, The, 190
Trail of '98, The, 106
Trail of the Vigilantes, The, 176, 184
Treasure of Silver Lake, The, 232
True Grit, 223, 239, 241
Tumbleweed, 211
Tumbleweeds, 43-45, 76
Tumbling Tumbleweeds, 146

Turpin, Dick, 66
Twenty Mule Team, 184
Two Gun Law, 131
Two Guns and a Badge, 213-14
Two Rode Together, 49
Tyler, Tom, 96, 129, 152

Uncensored Movies, 61, 68
Unforgiven, The, 226
Union Pacific, 72, 160, 166
Utah Kid, The, 129
Untamed Breed, The, 189

Valley of Fire, 206
Valley of Gold, 83
Valley of the Sun, 201
Van Dyke, W. S., 78, 90, 162
Vanishing American, The, 155, 180
Vidor, King, 109, 110, 112, 159, 160, 178, 199
Vigilantes Are Coming, The, 169
Virginia City, 176
Virginian, The, 54, 109, 178

Waco, 210
Wagonmaster, The, 201, 204, 241
Wagon Tracks, 70
Wakeley, Jimmy, 148, 191, 199
Wales, Wally, 84, 138
Walsh, Raoul, 109, 140, 196
Wanderer of the Wasteland, 198
Warhol, Andy, 234
War on the Plains, 29
Warren, James, 198
War Wagon, The, 234
Water for Canitoga, 177
Wayne, John, 3, 12, 47, 55, 110, 111, 119, 138, 152, 174, 184, 188, 222, 223, 239, 241
Way of the West, The, 138
Way Out West, 158
Wellman, William, 115, 154, 188, 196, 203
Wells Fargo, 72, 158, 165
Wells, Ted, 85
Western Union, 176, 178

West of the Pecos, 10, 136
When a Man's a Man, 132, 136
When the Daltons Rode, 181, 184
Whispering Smith, 54, 178
Whispering Smith Rides Again, 168
White Eagle, 130
White Feather, 216
White Gold, 102, 105
White, Pearl, 57, 167
Why the Sheriff Is a Bachelor, 65
Wichita, 213
Wild Bill Hickok, 42, 43, 44, 160, 164, 220
Wild Bill Hickok Rides, 185
Wild Blood, 105
Wild Bunch, The, 237-239
Wild Girl of the Sierras, The, 59
Wild West Days, 170
Willat, Irvin, 78
Williams, Big Boy, 125, 137
Will Penny, 241
Wilson, Whip, 191, 199
Winchester, 73, 203
Wind, The, 104
Winners of the Wilderness, 90
Winners of the West, 170
Winning of Barbara Worth, The, 78, 181
Wise, Robert, 184
With Sitting Bull at the Spirit Lake Massacre, 100
Witney, William, 190, 210
Woman, The, 33
Woman of the Town, The, 188
Woods, Harry, 230
Wyler, William, 78, 111, 178, 217
Wyoming, 6, 182
Wyoming Hurricane, 237

Xydias, Anthony J., 97

Yellow Sky, 188
Yodellin' Kid from Pine Ridge, 146

Zinneman, Fred, 206
Zorro's Black Whip, 10